Cursive Writing
for Right- and
Left-Handed Kids

An Effective Developmental Approach for All Children!

by
Sherrill B. Flora

illustrated by
Julie Anderson

Key Education®
An imprint of Carson-Dellosa Publishing LLC
Greensboro, North Carolina

carsondellosa.com

Credits
Author: Sherrill B. Flora
Illustrations: Julie Anderson
Editors: Claude Chalk and Karen Seberg
Cover Photography: © Comstock © Shutterstock

Key Education®
An imprint of Carson-Dellosa Publishing LLC
PO Box 35665
Greensboro, NC 27425 USA
carsondellosa.com

ISBN 978-160268-059-3
04-282178091

Contents

I. The Importance of Teaching Good Handwriting

Teaching good handwriting is a skill that has been neglected in many of our school systems. For example, with the increasing use of computers in the classroom, the teaching of keyboarding skills appears to have become a higher priority than the teaching of handwriting. Furthermore, many teachers are understandably feeling immense pressure to devote their time to teaching those subjects that will be tested. It also seems that many of todays younger teachers were not taught to pay as much attention to handwriting skills as teachers once did. Although we have witnessed a decline in handwriting skills—educators still know that good handwriting is as essential for academic success today as it was when our forefathers beautifully scripted their signatures on the Declaration of Independence.

Educational research has provided evidence that students who are not able to write legibly are at a serious disadvantage. This deficiency can result in lower grades when teachers are not able to read correct written responses. An illegible job application could be the direct cause of not being hired by an employer. Furthermore, it needs to be understood that good handwriting is a crucial tool for effective communication and personal expression.

Clear and legible handwriting skills are important for every aspect of learning.

❏ Handwriting is necessary for effective classroom note-taking, test-taking, and homework assignments.

❏ Good handwriting is still a requirement for many occupations.

❏ Good handwriting skills can help build self-esteem in children who may not perform as well in other academic areas.

❏ Proper letter formation has been linked to improved reading and spelling success. (See page 5, Handwriting Suggestions for Struggling Students and Special Learners.)

II. Effective Teaching Tips and Techniques

The following list provides the teacher with some helpful teaching tips and techniques to ensure that their students will have successful handwriting experiences.

❏ **Short Handwriting Classes.** To keep students motivated it is recommended that the handwriting class period only last from 10 to 15 minutes.

❏ **Initially Practice the Physical Movement.** When introducing a new series of letters that share a common stroke, such as the "Little Hill Letters," begin by teaching the movement of the stroke. Have the children move their arms through the air. Practice writing the stroke or letter in the air. Children also enjoy using water and a paintbrush to draw large stokes on a chalkboard.

❏ **Introduce Letters Slowly.** Follow the developmental sequence chart (page 7) and let children master a couple of letters at a time before moving on to a new set of letters.

❏ **Provide Close Supervision.** It is very difficult to "unteach" bad habits.

❏ **Arrow Cues.** Provide the children with copies of the chart on page 7. Looking at a letter with arrow cues can be beneficial in helping the children learn to follow the correct letter formation.

❏ **Teach Letter Connections.** Cursive writing requires making connections between letters. Do not teach letters in isolation. As soon as students can write even one letter, teach them how to connect and continuously write the letter several times. As soon as the students know several letters, have them practice writing words that can be spelled from those letters.

❏ **Pencil Grips.** Use pencil grips for children who have a difficult time remembering how to hold their pencil.

❏ **Short Pencils.** Break or sharpen pencils down to about a 2-inch length. This will encourage small hands to hold the pencil properly.

❏ **Chubby Writing Tools.** Use sidewalk chalk, chubby crayons, or a chubby pencil cut down to a short 2-inch length to help children gain more control.

❏ **Eventually Aim for Speed.** Although legible handwriting is the goal, students must eventually develop enough speed in order for their writing skills to become effective.

- ❏ **Your Own Style.** Once students have acquired legible handwriting with correct letter formation and accurate letter spacing, encourage them to develop a personal style that reflects their own personalities.

(Posture, Paper Alignment, and Pencil Grasp for Right-Handed Students, See section III. below for Specific Strategies for Left-Handed Students.)

- ❏ **Maintain Good Posture.** Feet should be on the floor and the desk surface should be at a height for the arm and elbow to rest comfortably. Ankles, hips, and knees should all be at 90 degree angles. If the chair is too high, place a foot stool under the child's feet.

- ❏ **Proper Pencil Grasp.** The pencil should be held between the pads of the thumb and the index finger while resting on the middle finger. Another appropriate version of this grasp is for the pencil to be held between the pads of the thumb and the index and middle fingers while resting on the ring finger.

- ❏ **Align Paper.** Be sure that the paper is aligned parallel to the arm of the dominant hand and is at a 45 degree angle. The left hand should be used to hold the paper stable.

III. Specific Strategies for Left-Handed Students

Left-handed students have many more challenges in learning how to write. First, the English language requires that we write from left to right—just like we read. This writing direction allows the right-handed writer to "pull" the pencil away from the body and moves fluently across the paper. The left-handed writer must "push" the pencil as the arm moves towards and across the body. Many left-handed people find themselves holding their pencils in a "hooked" position as they write. This "hooked" position generally occurs because what they are writing is hidden by their writing hand, and they are attempting not to smear their own writing. This handwriting style is not correct, can be physically uncomfortable, and may even cause illegible handwriting. Left-handed children need to be carefully TAUGHT how to write, taking into consideration the unique differences when writing with the left-hand. (See illustrations below.)

- ❏ **Maintain Good Posture.** (Same as above.)

- ❏ **Proper Pencil Grasp.** The pencil should be held between the pads of the thumb and the index finger while resting on the middle finger—approximately 1" (2 cm) to 1.5" (3.8 cm) from the point of the pencil.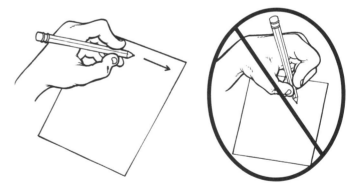

- ❏ **Align Paper.** The paper is slanted (about 20%) to the right —although this can vary depending on comfort.

- ❏ **Arm, Wrist, and Hand Position.** The wrist should be straight and below the writing line. The arm should be almost parallel with the paper.

- ❏ **Handwriting Slant.** The cursive letter slant usually taught is difficult for left-handed students. It is more natural and more comfortable for left-handed students to write letters using an upright slant or even slanting their letters slightly to the left. (See Left-Handed Writing Chart on page 7.)

IV. Handwriting Suggestions for Struggling Students and Special Learners

Good handwriting benefits all children, including those children with learning disabilities that involve handwriting difficulties. Although word processing programs and assistive technology are wonderful tools for children with writing problems, this technology should not eliminate the need for explicit handwriting instruction.

Good cursive handwriting instruction has been shown to assist in the development of reading and spelling skills of struggling students and special learners. In kindergarten, young children are typically taught how to "print." Then, when they reach the end of second grade, or in the beginning of third grade, children are taught cursive writing. Learning how to print and then having to switch to cursive handwriting creates another level of difficulty that can cause confusion. Being taught one method of continuous cursive handwriting is often recommend as the preferred handwriting system for these children.

Continuous cursive can be helpful for the following reasons:

❑ The continuous movement of cursive writing can decrease sequencing difficulties .

❑ By using continuous movement, a child can develop a "physical memory" of the word.

❑ Children are less likely to reverse letters which are typically difficult, such as "b and d" or "p and q," because of using continuous movement.

❑ There is a clearer distinction between uppercase and lowercase letters.

❑ The movement of writing from left to right also helps students see that letters are joined in a sequence that is more representational of how we blend the letter sounds as we read.

The following are some simple ideas that can be extremely beneficial for the students:

❑ **Use Graph Paper.** For struggling students, the use of graph paper can help them develop proper letter size and letter spacing.

❑ **Slanted Surface.** Placing a 4-inch three ring-binder on the desk in front of the child can sometimes be helpful. The spine of the binder should be facing the top of the desk. Rotate the binder to a 45 degree angle. Tape a piece of writing paper on the binder. Writing on this slanted surface is fun and can be extremely beneficial.

A special note about the learning disability called dysgraphia: There is a specific learning challenge known as dysgraphia—which literally means "difficulty with writing." Children who have dysgraphia may complain of cramped fingers while writing, erase excessively, write words backwards, experience trouble in sequencing the letters in words, have inconsistent letter formation, use a mixture of uppercase and lowercase letters, and their handwriting may be totally illegible. If you suspect dysgraphia, a more comprehensive multi-sensory therapy plan will be needed, and more than likely these children will eventually need to use computers and word processing programs when working on their writing skills.

V. Incorporate Sensory Integration Activities

Often children with illegible handwriting have a combination of problems, such as the inability to revisualize letters, and the inability to remember the motor patterns of letter forms. Sensory integration activities can help the brain process, organize, and interpret sensory input that can be extremely beneficial when practicing handwriting. Here are some easy-to-implement suggestions:

❑ Use a fingertip and practice on sandpaper.

❑ Fill a cookie sheet with sand or rice and then practice printing letters and words.

❑ Using a straight arm and pointed finger, pretend to write letters in the air (often called "sky-writing").

❑ Practice handwriting on a chalkboard using a paintbrush and water.

❑ Finger paint letters and words. Add glitter or salt to the paint to add an additional texture.

❑ Add various scents to finger paint, such as mint or lemon extract to add the sense of smell.

❑ Print letters and words on paper plates using edible substances, such as yogurt, peanut butter, and pudding.

❑ Have the children sit on chairs with comfortable padded seats or on large exercise balls.

❑ Write on the blackboard or on chart paper using wrist weights (make sure they are comfortable and not too heavy). The writing movements of the arm will feel more obvious when using the weights.

Right-Handed Letter Formation Chart & Sequence of Letter Introduction

Little Letters—Swing Up and Down

i t u w r s

Little Letters (with a tail)

p j

Little Round Letters—Swing Up, Curve Over, and Down

c o a d

Little Round Letters (with a tail)

g q

Little Hill Letters—Swing Up, Over, and Down

n m v x

Little Hill Letters (with a tail)

y z

Little Tall Letters— Swing Up and Back Around Letters

e l h b k f

Big Round Letters

C A O E

Big Flagpole Letters

N M K H

Big Letters with a Ball

P B R

Big Snake Letters

U W Y V X

Big Letters with a Hat

T F

Big Curly Letters

Q Z I J G S L D

Left-Handed Letter Formation Chart & Sequence of Letter Introduction

Little Letters—Swing Up and Down

i t u w r s

Little Letters (with a tail)

p j

Little Round Letters—Swing Up, Curve Over, and Down

c o a d

Little Round Letters (with a tail)

g q

Little Hill Letters—Swing Up, Over, and Down

n m v x

Little Hill Letters (with a tail)

y z

Little Tall Letters— Swing Up and Back Around Letters

e l h b k f

Big Round Letters

C A O E

Big Flagpole Letters

N M K H

Big Letters with a Ball

P B R

Big Snake Letters

U W Y V X

Big Letters with a Hat

T F

Big Curly Letters

Q Z I J G S L D

Introduction to Little Letters

i t u w r s p j

Name _____

All the little letters begin on the baseline. Put your pencil on the baseline and swing up and then down. Just like waves in the ocean! Start on the ● and end on the ■.

Introduction to Little Letters

i t u w r s p j

Name _____

All the little letters begin on the baseline. Put your pencil on the baseline and swing up and then down. Just like waves in the ocean! Start on the ● and end on the ■.

Trace the letters.

Name _____

Level 1 R

2

1

Rainbow Writing Directions: Trace each letter several times, each time using a different colored crayon.

Trace the letters.

Name _____

Level 1 R

2

1

Rainbow Writing Directions: Trace each letter several times, each time using a different colored crayon.

Level 1 L

Trace the letters.

Name _____

Rainbow Writing Directions: Trace each letter several times, each time using a different colored crayon.

Level 1 L

Trace the letters.

Name _____

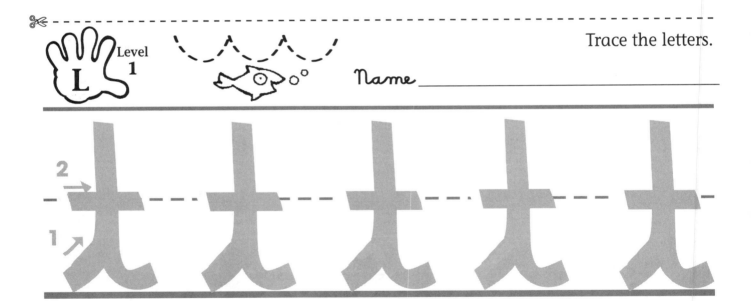

Rainbow Writing Directions: Trace each letter several times, each time using a different colored crayon.

Level 2 R

Learn Letters

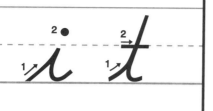

Name _____

The tiger tried to tumble.

Trace the letters.

i i i i i i i i i i

Cursive write the letters.   Circle your favorite letters.

Circle letters " i " and " t."

i t i u w t u i t

Trace the letters.

t t t t t t t t t t

Cursive write the letters.   Circle your favorite letters.

L Level 2

Name _____

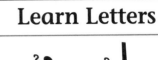

The tiger tried to tumble.

Learn Letters

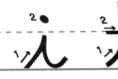

Trace the letters.

i i i i i i i i i i

Cursive write the letters.   Circle your favorite letters.

Circle letters "*i*" and "*t*."

i t i u w t u i t

Trace the letters.

Cursive write the letters.   Circle your favorite letters.

Level
3
R

Name _____

Trace the letters.   Cursive write the letters.

i i i i i i

Trace the words.

it iii tt it it it it

Cursive write the words.   Circle your favorites.

✂ -

Aa Bb Cc Dd Ee Ff Gg Hh Ii Jj Kk Ll Mm Nn Oo Pp Qq Rr Ss Tt Uu Vv Ww Xx Yy Zz

Level
3
R

Name _____

Trace the letters.   Cursive write the letters.

t t t t t t

Trace the words.

iii tt ttii it it it it

Cursive write the words.   Circle your favorites.

Level 3

Name _____

Trace the letters.

Cursive write the letters.

i i i i i i

Trace the words.

it iii tt it it it it

Cursive write the words.

Circle your favorites.

✂ -

Level 3

Name _____

Trace the letters.

Cursive write the letters.

t t t t t t

Trace the words.

iii tt ttii it it it it

Cursive write the words.

Circle your favorites.

Trace the letters.

Name _____

Level 1 **R**

Rainbow Writing Directions: Trace each letter several times, each time using a different colored crayon.

Trace the letters.

Name _____

Level 1 **R**

Rainbow Writing Directions: Trace each letter several times, each time using a different colored crayon.

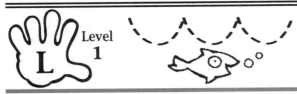

Level 1 L

Trace the letters.

Name _____

Rainbow Writing Directions: Trace each letter several times, each time using a different colored crayon.

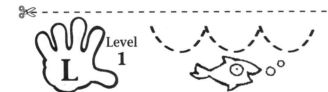

Rainbow Writing Directions: Trace each letter several times, each time using a different colored crayon.

Level 2 R

Learn Letters

u *w*

Name _____

The *wind* blew the *umbrella* up.

Trace the letters.

Cursive write the letters.   Circle your favorite letters.

Circle letters "*u*" and "*w*."

w *n* *u* *i* *w* *u* *t* *u* *w*

Trace the letters.

Cursive write the letters.   Circle your favorite letters.

L Level 2

Name _____

The wind blew the umbrella up.

Learn Letters

𝓊 𝓌

Trace the letters.

Cursive write the letters.   Circle your favorite letters.

Circle letters "𝓊" and "𝓌"

𝓌   𝓃   𝓊   𝒾   𝓌   𝓊   𝓉   𝓊   𝓌

Trace the letters.

Cursive write the letters.   Circle your favorite letters.

Level
3
R

u

Name _____

Trace the letters.

Cursive write the letters.

u   u   u   u   u

Trace the words.

ut   tiu   wit   wii   utur

Cursive write the words.

Circle your favorites.

✂ -

Level
3
R

w

Name _____

Trace the letters.

Cursive write the letters.

w   w   w   w

Trace the words.

wii   wit   uti   wiur   tui

Cursive write the words.

Circle your favorites.

(Little Letters)

Level 3

Name _____

Trace the letters.

Cursive write the letters.

u u u u u u

Trace the words.

ut tu wit wii utw

Cursive write the words.

Circle your favorites.

✂ -

Level 3

Name _____

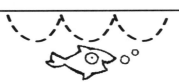

Trace the letters.

Cursive write the letters.

w w w w w

Trace the words.

wii wit uti wiw tui

Cursive write the words.

Circle your favorites.

Trace the letters.

Name _____

Level 1 R

r r r r

Rainbow Writing Directions: Trace each letter several times, each time using a different colored crayon.

Trace the letters.

Name _____

Level 1 R

s s s s

Rainbow Writing Directions: Trace each letter several times, each time using a different colored crayon.

L Level **1**

Trace the letters.

Name _____

Rainbow Writing Directions: Trace each letter several times, each time using a different colored crayon.

 **L** Level **1**

Trace the letters.

Name _____

Rainbow Writing Directions: Trace each letter several times, each time using a different colored crayon.

Level 2

R

Learn Letters

r s

Trace the letters.

Name _____

Lots of silly rabbits run races.

r r r r r r r r r r r

Cursive write the letters.

Circle your favorite letters.

Circle letters "*r*" and "*s*."

s i s w r s r u r

Trace the letters.

s s s s s s s s s

Cursive write the letters.

Circle your favorite letters.

L Level 2

Name _____

Lots of silly rabbits run races.

Learn Letters

r s

Trace the letters.

r r r r r r r r r

Cursive write the letters.   Circle your favorite letters.

Circle letters "r" and "s."

s i s w r s r u r

Trace the letters.

s s s s s s s s s

Cursive write the letters.   Circle your favorite letters.

Level 3 R

Name _____

Trace the letters.

Cursive write the letters.

r r r r r r

Trace the words.

rit sit rut tir wit

Cursive write the words.

Circle your favorites.

✂ -

Aa Bb Cc Dd Ee Ff Gg Hh Ii Jj Kk Ll Mm Nn Oo Pp Qq Rr Ss Tt Uu Vv Ww Xx Yy Zz

Level 3 R

Name _____

Trace the letters.

Cursive write the letters.

s s s s s s

Trace the words.

is tis sit sir it wit

Cursive write the words.

Circle your favorites.

Level 3

Aa Bb Cc Dd Ee Ff Gg Hh Ii Jj Kk Ll Mm Nn Oo Pp Qq Rr Ss Tt Uu Vv Ww Xx Yy Zz

Name _____

r

Trace the letters.

Cursive write the letters.

r r r r r r

Trace the words.

rit   sit   rut   tir   wit

Cursive write the words.

Circle your favorites.

✂ -

Level 3

Aa Bb Cc Dd Ee Ff Gg Hh Ii Jj Kk Ll Mm Nn Oo Pp Qq Rr Ss Tt Uu Vv Ww Xx Yy Zz

Name _____

s

Trace the letters.

Cursive write the letters.

s s s s s s

Trace the words.

is   tis   sit   sir   it   wit

Cursive write the words.

Circle your favorites.

Trace the letters.

Name _____

Level 1 R

Rainbow Writing Directions: Trace each letter several times, each time using a different colored crayon.

Trace the letters.

Name _____

Level 1 R

Rainbow Writing Directions: Trace each letter several times, each time using a different colored crayon.

Level 1

Trace the letters.

Name _____

Rainbow Writing Directions: Trace each letter several times, each time using a different colored crayon.

Level 1

Trace the letters.

Name _____

Rainbow Writing Directions: Trace each letter several times, each time using a different colored crayon.

Level 2 **R**

Learn Letters

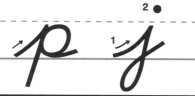

Name _____

The purple jay jumped rope.

Trace the letters.

Cursive write the letters.   Circle your favorite letters.

Circle letters "*p*" and "*j*."

j p s p t p w j j

Trace the letters.

Cursive write the letters.   Circle your favorite letters.

L Level 2

Name _____

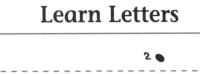

Learn Letters

p   *j*

The purple jay jumped rope.

Trace the letters.

Cursive write the letters.   Circle your favorite letters.

Circle letters "*p*" and "*j*."

j p s p t p w j j

Trace the letters.

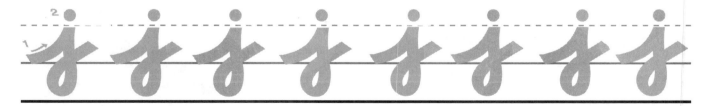

Cursive write the letters.   Circle your favorite letters.

Level 3 **R**

p

Name _____

Trace the letters.

Cursive write the letters.

p p p p p

Trace the words.

tip up wit sip pit

Cursive write the words.

Circle your favorites.

✂ -

Aa Bb Cc Dd Ee Ff Gg Hh Ii Jj Kk Ll Mm Nn Oo Pp Qq Rr Ss Tt Uu Vv Ww Xx Yy Zz

Level 3 **R**

2•
1 j

Name _____

Trace the letters.

Cursive write the letters.

j j j j j j

Trace the words.

jip pit sip up rip

Cursive write the words.

Circle your favorites.

Aa Bb Cc Dd Ee Ff Gg Hh Ii Jj Kk Ll Mm Nn Oo Pp 2q Rr Ss Tt Uu Vv Ww Xx Yy Zz

Name _____

Trace the letters.

Cursive write the letters.

p p p p p p

Trace the words.

tip up wit sip pit

Cursive write the words.

Circle your favorites.

Aa Bb Cc Dd Ee Ff Gg Hh Ii Jj Kk Ll Mm Nn Oo Pp 2q Rr Ss Tt Uu Vv Ww Xx Yy Zz

Name _____

Trace the letters.

Cursive write the letters.

j j j j j j

Trace the words.

jip pit sup up rip

Cursive write the words.

Circle your favorites.

Cursive Writing for Right- and Left-Handed Kids

Aa Bb Cc Dd Ee Ff Gg Hh Ii Jj Kk Ll Mm Nn Oo Pp Qq Rr Ss Tt Uu Vv Ww Xx Yy Zz

Review Little Letters

R

i t u w r s p j

Name _____

Trace the letters.

i t u w r s p j

Cursive write the letters.

Circle your favorites.

Trace the words.

it pit rut sup wit jip

Cursive write the words.

Circle your favorites.

Aa Bb Cc Dd Ee Ff Gg Hh Ii Jj Kk Ll Mm Nn Oo Pp Qq Rr Ss Tt Uu Vv Ww Xx Yy Zz

L

Review Little Letters

Name _____

i t u w r s p j

Trace the letters.

i t u w r s p j

Cursive write the letters.

Circle your favorites.

Trace the words.

it pit rut sup wit jip

Cursive write the words.

Circle your favorites.

Name _____

Introduction to Little Round Letters

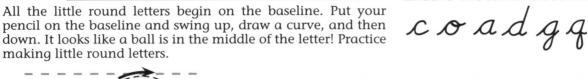

All the little round letters begin on the baseline. Put your pencil on the baseline and swing up, draw a curve, and then down. It looks like a ball is in the middle of the letter! Practice making little round letters.

✂ -

Aa Bb Cc Dd Ee Ff Gg Hh Ii Jj Kk Ll Mm Nn Oo Pp 2q Rr Ss Tt Uu Vv Ww Xx Yy Zz

Introduction to Little Round Letters

Name _____

All the little round letters begin on the baseline. Put your pencil on the baseline and swing up, draw a curve, and then down. It looks like a ball is in the middle of the letter! Practice making little round letters.

Trace the letters.

Name _____

Level
1
R

c c c c

Rainbow Writing Directions: Trace each letter several times, each time using a different colored crayon.

Trace the letters.

Name _____

Level
1
R

o o o o

Rainbow Writing Directions: Trace each letter several times, each time using a different colored crayon.

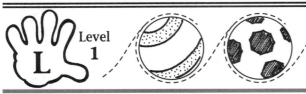

Level 1

Trace the letters.

Name _____

c c c c

Rainbow Writing Directions: Trace each letter several times, each time using a different colored crayon.

Level 1

Trace the letters.

Name _____

e e e e

Rainbow Writing Directions: Trace each letter several times, each time using a different colored crayon.

Level 2 **R**

Learn Letters

c *o*

Name _____

The *octopus* *could* open the *can*.

Trace the letters.

c c c c c c c c c c

Cursive write the letters.   Circle your favorite letters.

Circle letters "*c*" and "*o*."

c o a s o o c u c

Trace the letters.

o o o o o o o o o o o

Cursive write the letters.   Circle your favorite letters.

Level **L** 2

Name _____

Learn Letters

C O

The octopus could open the can.

Trace the letters.

c c c c c c c c c c c

Cursive write the letters.   Circle your favorite letters.

Circle letters "c" and "o."

c o a s o o c u c

Trace the letters.

o o o o o o o o o o o

Cursive write the letters.   Circle your favorite letters.

Level 3 **R**

c

Name _____

Trace the letters.

Cursive write the letters.

c c c c c c

Trace the words.

tip cup pic cut puc

Cursive write the words.

Circle your favorites.

✂ -

Aa Bb Cc Dd Ee Ff Gg Hh Ii Jj Kk Ll Mm Nn Oo Pp Qq Rr Ss Tt Uu Vv Ww Xx Yy Zz

Level 3 **R**

o

Name _____

Trace the letters.

Cursive write the letters.

o o o o o o

Trace the words.

top cop pot cour pop

Cursive write the words.

Circle your favorites.

Name _____

Trace the letters.   Cursive write the letters.

c c c c c c

Trace the words.

tip cup pic cut puc

Cursive write the words.   Circle your favorites.

✂ -

Name _____

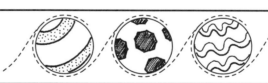

Trace the letters.   Cursive write the letters.

o o o o o o

Trace the words.

top cop pot cow pop

Cursive write the words.   Circle your favorites.

Trace the letters.

Name _____

Level 1 R

a a a a

Rainbow Writing Directions: Trace each letter several times, each time using a different colored crayon.

Trace the letters.

Name _____

Level 1 R

d d d d

Rainbow Writing Directions: Trace each letter several times, each time using a different colored crayon.

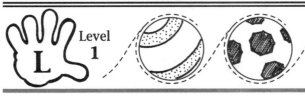

Aa Bb Cc Dd Ee Ff Gg Hh Ii Jj Kk Ll Mm Nn Oo Pp Qq Rr Ss Tt Uu Vv Ww Xx Yy Zz

(Little Round Letters)

Level 1 — L

Trace the letters.

Name _____

a a a a

Rainbow Writing Directions: Trace each letter several times, each time using a different colored crayon.

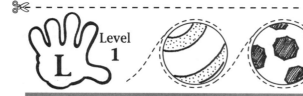

Level 1 — L

Trace the letters.

Name _____

d d d d

Rainbow Writing Directions: Trace each letter several times, each time using a different colored crayon.

KE-804073 © Carson-Dellosa

Cursive Writing for Right- and Left-Handed Kids

Level 2 **R**

Learn Letters

a d

Name _____

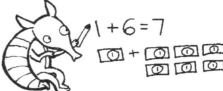

1 + 6 = 7

Addie is adding all the dollars.

Trace the letters.

a a a a a a a a a a a

Cursive write the letters.   Circle your favorite letters.

- - - - - - - - - - - - - - - - - - -

Circle letters "*a*" and "*d*."

a p s d a d d o a

Trace the letters.

d d d d d d d d d d d

Cursive write the letters.   Circle your favorite letters.

- - - - - - - - - - - - - - - - - - -

L Level 2

Name _____

1 + 6 = 7

Addie is adding all the dollars.

Learn Letters

a d

Trace the letters.

a a a a a a a a a a a

Cursive write the letters.

Circle your favorite letters.

Circle letters "a" and "d."

a p s d a d d o a

Trace the letters.

d d d d d d d d d d d

Cursive write the letters.

Circle your favorite letters.

Level 3 **R**

a

Name _____

Trace the letters.   Cursive write the letters.

a a a a a a

Trace the words.

sat cap was at pass

Cursive write the words.   Circle your favorites.

Level 3 **R**

d

Name _____

Trace the letters.   Cursive write the letters.

d d d d d d

Trace the words.

toad coat soap wood

Cursive write the words.   Circle your favorites.

L Level 3

Name _____

Trace the letters.   Cursive write the letters.

a a a a a a a

Trace the words.

sat cap was at pass

Cursive write the words.   Circle your favorites.

✂ -

L Level 3

Aa Bb Cc Dd Ee Ff Gg Hh Ii Jj Kk Ll Mm Nn Oo Pp Qq Rr Ss Tt Uu Vv Ww Xx Yy Zz

Name _____

d

Trace the letters.   Cursive write the letters.

d d d d d d

Trace the words.

toad coat soap wood

Cursive write the words.   Circle your favorites.

Trace the letters.

Name _____

Level 1 R

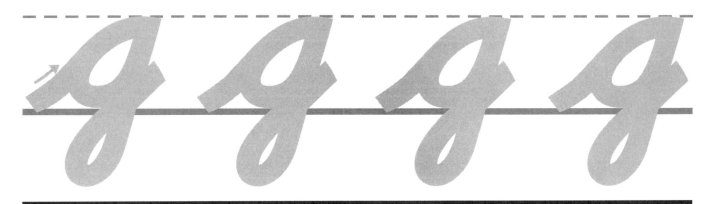

Rainbow Writing Directions: Trace each letter several times, each time using a different colored crayon.

Trace the letters.

Name _____

Level 1 R

Rainbow Writing Directions: Trace each letter several times, each time using a different colored crayon.

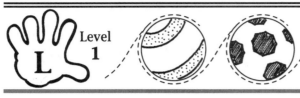 Level 1

Trace the letters.

Name _____

Rainbow Writing Directions: Trace each letter several times, each time using a different colored crayon.

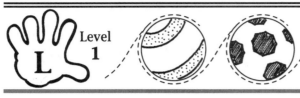 Level 1

Trace the letters.

Name _____

Rainbow Writing Directions: Trace each letter several times, each time using a different colored crayon.

Level 2 R

Learn Letters

g   g

Name _____

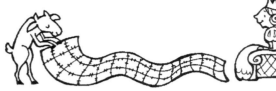

The quiet goat got the queen's quilt.

Trace the letters.

g g g g g g g g g

Cursive write the letters.

Circle your favorite letters.

Circle letters "*g*" and "*q*."

q p p g g g d g g j

Trace the letters.

g g g g g g g g g

Cursive write the letters.

Circle your favorite letters.

Level L 2

Name _____

Learn Letters

g *q*

The quiet goat got the queen's quilt.

Trace the letters.

g g g g g g g g g g

Cursive write the letters.   Circle your favorite letters.

Circle letters " *g* " and " *q*."

q p q g g d q g j

Trace the letters.

q q q q q q q q q q

Cursive write the letters.   Circle your favorite letters.

(Little Round Letters with a Tail)

Level 3 R

g

Name _____

Trace the letters.   Cursive write the letters.

g g g g g g

Trace the words.

rug pug dig dog goat

Cursive write the words.   Circle your favorites.

✂ -

Level 3 R

q

Name _____

Trace the letters.   Cursive write the letters.

q q q q q q

Trace the words.

quit rust quite squid

Cursive write the words.   Circle your favorites.

Aa Bb Cc Dd Ee Ff Gg Hh Ii Jj Kk Ll Mm Nn Oo Pp Qq Rr Ss Tt Uu Vv Ww Xx Yy Zz

Level 3

Name _____

g

Trace the letters.

Cursive write the letters.

g g g g g g

Trace the words.

rug pug dig dog goat

Cursive write the words.

Circle your favorites.

Aa Bb Cc Dd Ee Ff Gg Hh Ii Jj Kk Ll Mm Nn Oo Pp Qq Rr Ss Tt Uu Vv Ww Xx Yy Zz

Level 3

Name _____

q

Trace the letters.

Cursive write the letters.

q q q q q q

Trace the words.

quit rust quite squid

Cursive write the words.

Circle your favorites.

**Review Little
Round Letters**

R

c o a d g q

Name _____

Trace the letters.

c o a d g q c o a d g q

Cursive write the letters.   Circle your favorites.

Trace the words.

coat quit dig pug squat

Cursive write the words.   Circle your favorites.

✂ -

L

**Review Little
Round Letters**

c o a d g q

Name _____

Trace the letters.

c o a d g q c o a d g q

Cursive write the letters.   Circle your favorites.

Trace the words.

coat quit dig pug squat

Cursive write the words.   Circle your favorites.

Name _____

All the little letters begin on the baseline. Put your pencil on the baseline and swing up, over, and then down. Just like little ants marching up, over, and down an ant hill!

Introduction to Little Hill Letters

n m v x y z

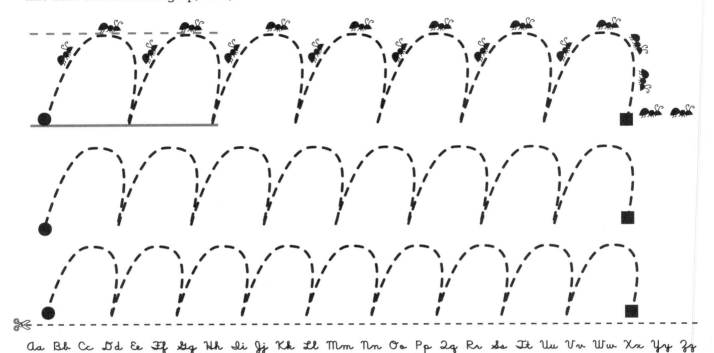

Introduction to Little Hill Letters

n m v x y z

Name _____

All the little letters begin on the baseline. Put your pencil on the baseline and swing up, over, and then down. Just like little ants marching up, over, and down an ant hill!

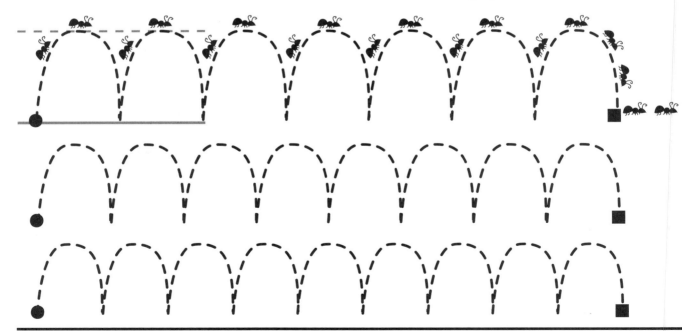

Trace the letters.

Name _____

Level 1 R

Rainbow Writing Directions: Trace each letter several times, each time using a different colored crayon.

Trace the letters.

Name _____

Level 1 R

Rainbow Writing Directions: Trace each letter several times, each time using a different colored crayon.

Level 1 **L**  Name _____

Trace the letters.

Rainbow Writing Directions: Trace each letter several times, each time using a different colored crayon.

Level 1 **L**  Name _____

Trace the letters.

Rainbow Writing Directions: Trace each letter several times, each time using a different colored crayon.

Level 2 **R**

Learn Letters

Name _____

Nine *mice* *mu*nched the *yu*mmy *n*achos.

Trace the letters.

𝓃 𝓃 𝓃 𝓃 𝓃 𝓃 𝓃 𝓃 𝓃 𝓃

Cursive write the letters.   Circle your favorite letters.

Circle letters "𝓃" and "𝓂."

𝓂 𝓃 𝓂 𝓊 𝓃 𝓃 𝓌 𝓂 𝒾

Trace the letters.

𝓂 𝓂 𝓂 𝓂 𝓂 𝓂 𝓂 𝓂 𝓂 𝓂

Cursive write the letters.   Circle your favorite letters.

L Level 2

Name _____

Nine mice munched the yummy nachos.

Learn Letters

m m

Trace the letters.

Cursive write the letters.   Circle your favorite letters.

Circle letters "m" and "m."

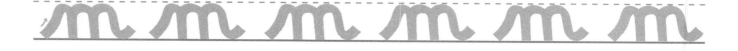

Trace the letters.

Cursive write the letters.   Circle your favorite letters.

Level 3 R

Trace the letters.

Cursive write the letters.

n n n n n

Trace the words.

an now ran spin

Cursive write the words.

Circle your favorites.

✂ -

Aa Bb Cc Dd Ee Ff Gg Hh Ii Jj Kk Ll Mm Nn Oo Pp 2q Rr Ss Tt Uu Vv Ww Xx Yy Zg

Level 3 R

Trace the letters.

Cursive write the letters.

m m m m m m

Trace the words.

arm made man jam

Cursive write the words.

Circle your favorites.

(Little Hill Letters)

Aa Bb Cc Dd Ee Ff Gg Hh Ii Jj Kk Ll Mm Nn Oo Pp Qq Rr Ss Tt Uu Vv Ww Xx Yy Zz

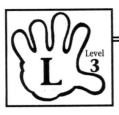

L Level **3**

Name _____

Trace the letters.

Cursive write the letters.

n n n n n

Trace the words.

an now ran spin

Cursive write the words.

Circle your favorites.

Aa Bb Cc Dd Ee Ff Gg Hh Ii Jj Kk Ll Mm Nn Oo Pp Qq Rr Ss Tt Uu Vv Ww Xx Yy Zz

L Level **3**

Name _____

Trace the letters.

Cursive write the letters.

m m m m m

Trace the words.

arm made man jam

Cursive write the words.

Circle your favorites.

Trace the letters.

Name _____

Level 1 R

Rainbow Writing Directions: Trace each letter several times, each time using a different colored crayon.

Trace the letters.

Name _____

Level 1 R

Rainbow Writing Directions: Trace each letter several times, each time using a different colored crayon.

Level 1

Trace the letters.

Name _____

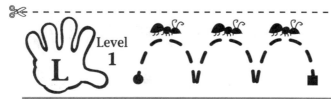

Rainbow Writing Directions: Trace each letter several times, each time using a different colored crayon.

Level 1

Trace the letters.

Name _____

Rainbow Writing Directions: Trace each letter several times, each time using a different colored crayon.

Level 2 **R**

Learn Letters

Name _____

A fox sat on a very little box with a violin.

Trace the letters.

Cursive write the letters.   Circle your favorite letters.

Circle letters "N" and "X."

Trace the letters.

Cursive write the letters.   Circle your favorite letters.

Level 2 L

Name _____

Learn Letters

A fox sat on a very little box with a violin.

Trace the letters.

Cursive write the letters.   Circle your favorite letters.

Circle letters "N" and "X."

N   X   U   W   X   X   N   M   N

Trace the letters.

Cursive write the letters.   Circle your favorite letters.

Level 3 R

Name _____

Trace the letters.

Cursive write the letters.

v v v v v

Trace the words.

van vet vow vast

Cursive write the words.

Circle your favorites.

Level 3 R

Name _____

Trace the letters.

Cursive write the letters.

x x x x x

Trace the words.

six mix wax taxi

Cursive write the words.

Circle your favorites.

Name _____

Trace the letters.   Cursive write the letters.

v v v v v

Trace the words.

van vet vow vast

Cursive write the words.   Circle your favorites.

✂ -

Name _____

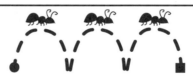

Trace the letters.   Cursive write the letters.

x x x x x

Trace the words.

six mix wax taxi

Cursive write the words.   Circle your favorites.

(Little Hill Letters with a Tail)

Aa Bb Cc Dd Ee Ff Gg Hh Ii Jj Kk Ll Mm Nn Oo Pp $2g$ Rr Ss Tt Uu Vv Ww Xx Yy Zz

Trace the letters.

Name _____

Level 1 **R**

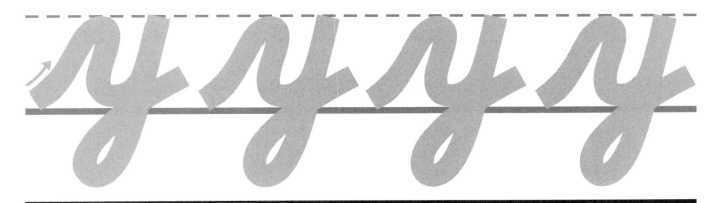

Rainbow Writing Directions: Trace each letter several times, each time using a different colored crayon.

Trace the letters.

Name _____

Level 1 **R**

Rainbow Writing Directions: Trace each letter several times, each time using a different colored crayon.

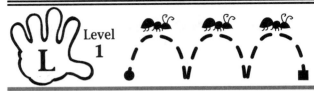

Level 1

L

Name _____

Trace the letters.

Rainbow Writing Directions: Trace each letter several times, each time using a different colored crayon.

Level 1

L

Name _____

Trace the letters.

Rainbow Writing Directions: Trace each letter several times, each time using a different colored crayon.

Level
2
R

Learn Letters

Name _____

At the zoo, the yak yawned
and zipped his yellow coat.

Y   Z

Trace the letters.

Y Y Y Y Y Y Y Y Y Y Y Y

Cursive write the letters.   Circle your favorite letters.

Circle letters " y " and " z ."

Z Z Y P Z Y j Y Z q

Trace the letters.

Z Z Z Z Z Z Z Z Z Z Z Z

Cursive write the letters.   Circle your favorite letters.

L Level 2

Name _____

At the zoo, the yak yawned
and zipped his yellow coat.

Learn Letters

Yy   Zz

Trace the letters.

Cursive write the letters.   Circle your favorite letters.

Circle letters "Yy" and "Zz."

Zz Yy Pp Zz Yy Jj Yy Zz Qq

Trace the letters.

Cursive write the letters.   Circle your favorite letters.

Level 3 R

Y

Name _____

Trace the letters.

Cursive write the letters.

y y y y y

Trace the words.

ray way yo-yo yarn

Cursive write the words.

Circle your favorites.

Level 3 R

Z

Name _____

Trace the letters.

Cursive write the letters.

z z z z z

Trace the words.

zip zap quiz zoom

Cursive write the words.

Circle your favorites.

Aa Bb Cc Dd Ee Ff Gg Hh Ii Jj Kk Ll Mm Nn Oo Pp 2q Rr Ss Tt Uu Vv Ww Xx Yy Zz

Name _____

Trace the letters.   Cursive write the letters.

Trace the words.

Cursive write the words.   Circle your favorites.

✂ -

Aa Bb Cc Dd Ee Ff Gg Hh Ii Jj Kk Ll Mm Nn Oo Pp 2q Rr Ss Tt Uu Vv Ww Xx Yy Zz

Name _____

Trace the letters.   Cursive write the letters.

Trace the words.

Cursive write the words.   Circle your favorites.

Aa Bb Cc Dd Ee Ff Gg Hh Ii Jj Kk Ll Mm Nn Oo Pp Qq Rr Ss Tt Uu Vv Ww Xx Yy Zz

Review
Little Hill Letters
R

n m v x y z

Name _____

Trace the letters.

n   m   v   x   y   z

Cursive write the letters.   Circle your favorites.

- -

Trace the words.

mine axe zap yak vine

Cursive write the words.   Circle your favorites.

- -

✂ -

L
Aa Bb Cc Dd Ee Ff Gg Hh Ii Jj Kk Ll Mm Nn Oo Pp Qq Rr Ss Tt Uu Vv Ww Xx Yy Zz

Review
Little Hill Letters
n m v x y z Name _____

Trace the letters.

n   m   v   x   y   z

Cursive write the letters.   Circle your favorites.

- -

Trace the words.

mine axe zap yak vine

Cursive write the words.   Circle your favorites.

- -

Name _____

Introduction to Little Tall Letters

e l h b k f

To write little tall letters, begin by putting your pencil on the baseline. Then, swing the line up and back around—making a big loop!

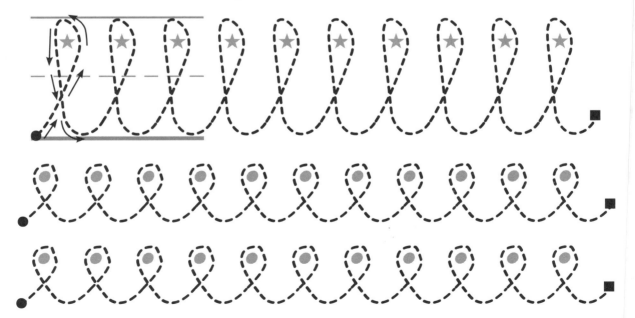

Introduction to Little Tall Letters

e l h b k f

Name _____

To write little tall letters, begin by putting your pencil on the baseline. Then, swing the line up and back around—making a big loop!

Trace the letters.

Name _____

Level 1

R

Rainbow Writing Directions: Trace each letter several times, each time using a different colored crayon.

Trace the letters.

Name _____

Level 1

R

Rainbow Writing Directions: Trace each letter several times, each time using a different colored crayon.

Level 1

Trace the letters.

Name _____

Rainbow Writing Directions: Trace each letter several times, each time using a different colored crayon.

Level 1

Trace the letters.

Name _____

Rainbow Writing Directions: Trace each letter several times, each time using a different colored crayon.

Level 2 **R**

Learn Letters

e l

Name _____

Ellie the elephant eats lots of eggplant.

Trace the letters.

e e e e e e e e e e e e e e

Cursive write the letters.   Circle your favorite letters.

Circle letters "*e*" and "*l*."

c l e l t o l e e

Trace the letters.

l l l l l l l l l l l l l l

Cursive write the letters.   Circle your favorite letters.

L Level 2

Name _____

Aa Bb Cc Dd Ee Ff Gg Hh Ii Jj Kk Ll Mm Nn Oo Pp Qq Rr Ss Tt Uu Vv Ww Xx Yy Zz

(Little Tall Letters)

Ellie the elephant eats lots of eggplant.

Learn Letters

e l

Trace the letters.

Cursive write the letters.   Circle your favorite letters.

Circle letters "e" and "l."

c l e l t o l e e

Trace the letters.

Cursive write the letters.   Circle your favorite letters.

Level 3 **R**

e

Name _____

Trace the letters.   Cursive write the letters.

e e e e e e

Trace the words.

even eye vase zero

Cursive write the words.   Circle your favorites.

✂ -

Level 3 **R**

l

Name _____

Trace the letters.   Cursive write the letters.

l l l l l l

Trace the words.

let cold only lazy

Cursive write the words.   Circle your favorites.

(Little Tall Letters)

Level 3

Name _____

Trace the letters.

Cursive write the letters.

e e e e e e

Trace the words.

even eye rase zero

Cursive write the words.

Circle your favorites.

Level 3

Name _____

Trace the letters.

Cursive write the letters.

l l l l l l

Trace the words.

let cold only lazy

Cursive write the words.

Circle your favorites.

Trace the letters.

Name _____

Level 1 R

Rainbow Writing Directions: Trace each letter several times, each time using a different colored crayon.

Trace the letters.

Name _____

Level 1 R

Rainbow Writing Directions: Trace each letter several times, each time using a different colored crayon.

Level 1   **L**

Trace the letters.

Name _____

Rainbow Writing Directions: Trace each letter several times, each time using a different colored crayon.

Level 1   **L**

Trace the letters.

Name _____

Rainbow Writing Directions: Trace each letter several times, each time using a different colored crayon.

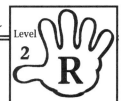

Level 2 R

Learn Letters

h b

Name _____

The bunny has a blue hat on her head.

Trace the letters.

h h h h h h h h h h

Cursive write the letters.   Circle your favorite letters.

Circle letters "h" and "b."

h k h b h t b b l

Trace the letters.

b b b b b b b b b b

Cursive write the letters.   Circle your favorite letters.

Aa Bb Cc Dd Ee Ff Gg Hh Ii Jj Kk Ll Mm Nn Oo Pp Qq Rr Ss Tt Uu Vv Ww Xx Yy Zz

(Little Tall Letters)

L Level 2

Name _____

Learn Letters

h b

The bunny has a blue hat on her head.

Trace the letters.

h h h h h h h h h

Cursive write the letters.   Circle your favorite letters.

Circle letters "h" and "b."

h k h b h t b b l

Trace the letters.

b b b b b b b b b

Cursive write the letters.   Circle your favorite letters.

Level
3
R

h

Name _____

Trace the letters.

Cursive write the letters.

h h h h h

Trace the words.

has hand hurt help

Cursive write the words.

Circle your favorites.

✂ -

Level
3
R

b

Name _____

Trace the letters.

Cursive write the letters.

b b b b b

Trace the words.

bite bee bank best bag

Cursive write the words.

Circle your favorites.

Aa Bb Cc Dd Ee Ff Gg Hh Ii Jj Kk Ll Mm Nn Oo Pp Qq Rr Ss Tt Uu Vv Ww Xx Yy Zz

Level 3

Name _____

Trace the letters.

Cursive write the letters.

h h h h h

Trace the words.

has hand hurt help

Cursive write the words.

Circle your favorites.

✂ -

Aa Bb Cc Dd Ee Ff Gg Hh Ii Jj Kk Ll Mm Nn Oo Pp Qq Rr Ss Tt Uu Vv Ww Xx Yy Zz

Level 3

Name _____

Trace the letters.

Cursive write the letters.

b b b b b

Trace the words.

bite bee bank best bag

Cursive write the words.

Circle your favorites.

 Cursive Writing for Right- and Left-Handed Kids

Trace the letters.

Name _____

Rainbow Writing Directions: Trace each letter several times, each time using a different colored crayon.

Trace the letters.

Name _____

Rainbow Writing Directions: Trace each letter several times, each time using a different colored crayon.

Level 1 L

Trace the letters.

Name _____

Rainbow Writing Directions: Trace each letter several times, each time using a different colored crayon.

Level 1 L

Trace the letters.

Name _____

Rainbow Writing Directions: Trace each letter several times, each time using a different colored crayon.

Learn Letters

Name _____

The fox kicked the football.

Trace the letters.

Cursive write the letters.   Circle your favorite letters.

Circle letters "k" and "f."

b k l k f f k f h

Trace the letters.

Cursive write the letters.   Circle your favorite letters.

L Level 2

Name _____

Learn Letters

k f

The fox kicked
the football.

Trace the letters.

Cursive write the letters.   Circle your favorite letters.

Circle letters "k" and "f."

b k l k f f k f h

Trace the letters.

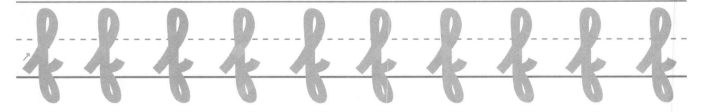

Cursive write the letters.   Circle your favorite letters.

Level 3 R

Name _____

Trace the letters.

Cursive write the letters.

k k k k k k

Trace the words.

keg key kite rake elk

Cursive write the words.

Circle your favorites.

Level 3 R

Name _____

Trace the letters.

Cursive write the letters.

f f f f f f

Trace the words.

fun frog fish off safe

Cursive write the words.

Circle your favorites.

Name _____

Trace the letters.

Cursive write the letters.

k k k k k k

Trace the words.

keg key kite rake elk

Cursive write the words.

Circle your favorites.

✂ -

Name _____

Trace the letters.

Cursive write the letters.

f f f f f f

Trace the words.

fun frog fish off safe

Cursive write the words.

Circle your favorites.

Aa Bb Cc Dd Ee Ff Gg Hh Ii Jj Kk Ll Mm Nn Oo Pp Qq Rr Ss Tt Uu Vv Ww Xx Yy Zz

Review
Little Tall Letters
e l h b k f

Name _____

Trace the letters.

e l h b k f e l h b k f

Cursive write the letters.   Circle your favorites.

Trace the words.

eel lad hut bop elk after

Cursive write the words.   Circle your favorites.

✂ -

Aa Bb Cc Dd Ee Ff Gg Hh Ii Jj Kk Ll Mm Nn Oo Pp Qq Rr Ss Tt Uu Vv Ww Xx Yy Zz

Review
Little Tall Letters
e l h b k f

Name _____

Trace the letters.

e l h b k f e l h b k f

Cursive write the letters.   Circle your favorites.

Trace the words.

eel lad hut bop elk after

Cursive write the words.   Circle your favorites.

Name _____

C a O E

All the big round letters begin as if you were going to print a "C" or draw a circle. Put your pencil on the ○ and end on the ●. Practice by drawing some circles.

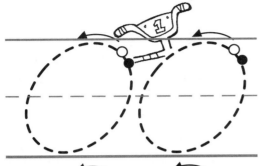

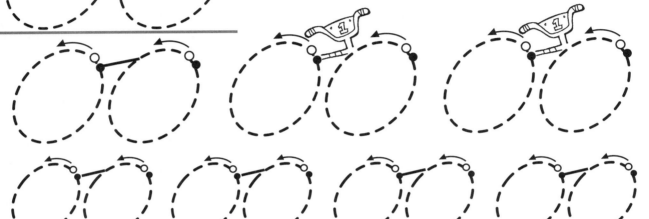

- - - - - - - - ✂ -

Name _____

C a O E

All the big round letters begin as if you were going to print a "C" or draw an oval. Put your pencil on the ○ and end on the ●. Practice by drawing some ovals.

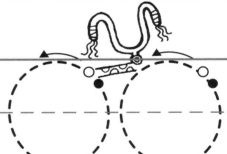

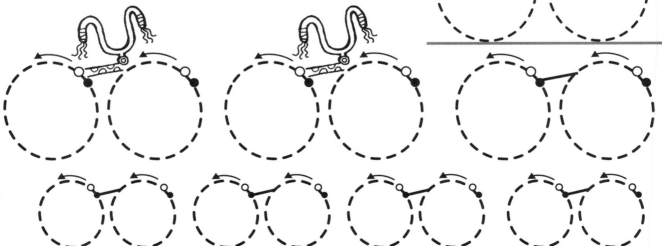

Trace the letters.

Name _____

Level 1 **R**

C C C C

Rainbow Writing Directions: Trace each letter several times, each time using a different colored crayon.

Trace the letters.

Name _____

Level 1 **R**

a a a a

Rainbow Writing Directions: Trace each letter several times, each time using a different colored crayon.

Level 1

Trace the letters.

Name _____

C C C C

Rainbow Writing Directions: Trace each letter several times, each time using a different colored crayon.

Level 1

Trace the letters.

Name _____

a a a a

Rainbow Writing Directions: Trace each letter several times, each time using a different colored crayon.

Level 2 **R**

Learn Letters

C a

Name _____

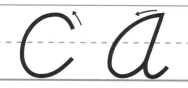

Cally Crocodile
and Alice Ant are friends.

Trace the letters.

C C C C C C C C C

Cursive write the letters.   Circle your favorite letters.

Circle letters "C" and "a."

C a a O C 2 C P a

Trace the letters.

a a a a a a a a a

Cursive write the letters.   Circle your favorite letters.

Level
L 2

Name _____

Cally Crocodile
and Alice Ant are friends.

Learn Letters

C a

Trace the letters.

C C C C C C C C C

Cursive write the letters.   Circle your favorite letters.

Circle letters " C " and "a ."

c a a o c 2 c p a

Trace the letters.

a a a a a a a a a

Cursive write the letters.   Circle your favorite letters.

Level **3** **R**

C

Name _____

Trace the letters.   Cursive write the letters.

C   C   C   C   C   C

Trace the words.

Cat   Carl   Cart   Carrot

Cursive write the words.   Circle your favorites.

- -

Aa Bb Cc Dd Ee Ff Gg Hh Ii Jj Kk Ll Mm Nn Oo Pp Qq Rr Ss Tt Uu Vv Ww Xx Yy Zz

Level **3** **R**

a

Name _____

Trace the letters.   Cursive write the letters.

a   a   a   a   a

Trace the words.

Ann   Ant   Apple   Ate

Cursive write the words.   Circle your favorites.

Aa Bb Cc Dd Ee Ff Gg Hh Ii Jj Kk Ll Mm Nn Oo Pp 2q Rr Ss Tt Uu Vv Ww Xx Yy Zz

Name _____

C

Trace the letters.

Cursive write the letters.

C C C C C C

Trace the words.

Cat Carl Cart Carrot

Cursive write the words.

Circle your favorites.

Aa Bb Cc Dd Ee Ff Gg Hh Ii Jj Kk Ll Mm Nn Oo Pp 2q Rr Ss Tt Uu Vv Ww Xx Yy Zz

Name _____

a

Trace the letters.

Cursive write the letters.

a a a a a

Trace the words.

Ann Ant Apple Ate

Cursive write the words.

Circle your favorites.

Trace the letters.

Name _____

Level 1 **R**

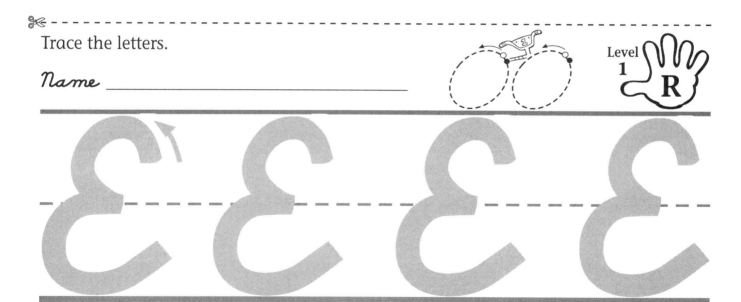

OOOO

Rainbow Writing Directions: Trace each letter several times, each time using a different colored crayon.

✂ -

Trace the letters.

Name _____

Level 1 **R**

EEEE

Rainbow Writing Directions: Trace each letter several times, each time using a different colored crayon.

(Big Round Letters)

Aa Bb Cc Dd Ee Ff Gg Hh Ii Jj Kk Ll Mm Nn Oo Pp Qq Rr Ss Tt Uu Vv Ww Xx Yy Zz

 Level 1

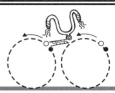

Trace the letters.

Name _____

Rainbow Writing Directions: Trace each letter several times, each time using a different colored crayon.

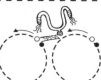 Level 1

Trace the letters.

Name _____

Rainbow Writing Directions: Trace each letter several times, each time using a different colored crayon.

Level 2 **R**

Learn Letters

O E

Name _____

This is Ollie Owl and Ed Eagle.

Trace the letters.

O O O O O O O O O

Cursive write the letters.

Circle your favorite letters.

Circle letters "O" and "E."

O C O E 2 O E A E

Trace the letters.

E E E E E E E E E

Cursive write the letters.

Circle your favorite letters.

Level 2

Name _____

This is Ollie Owl and Ed Eagle.

Learn Letters

O E

Trace the letters.

O O O O O O O O O

Cursive write the letters.   Circle your favorite letters.

Circle letters "O" and "E."

O C O E 2 O E a E

Trace the letters.

E E E E E E E E E

Cursive write the letters.   Circle your favorite letters.

Level 3 R

O

Name _____

Trace the letters.   Cursive write the letters.

O O O O O

Trace the words.

Owl   Ollie   Oscar   Oh!

Cursive write the words.   Circle your favorites.

✁- -

Level 3 R

E

Name _____

Trace the letters.   Cursive write the letters.

E E E E E

Trace the words.

Eddie   Edith   Exit   Enter

Cursive write the words.   Circle your favorites.

Name _____

Trace the letters.

Cursive write the letters.

O O O O O

Trace the words.

Owl Ollie Oscar Oh!

Cursive write the words.

Circle your favorites.

✂ -

Name _____

Trace the letters.

Cursive write the letters.

E E E E E

Trace the words.

Eddie Edith Exit Enter

Cursive write the words.

Circle your favorites.

Review
Big Round Letters
R

C a O E

Name _____

Trace the letters.

C C C a a a O O O E E E

Cursive write the letters.   Circle your favorites.

Trace the words.

Cal Allen Ollie Enter

Cursive write the words.   Circle your favorites.

L

Review
Big Round Letters

C a O E

Name _____

Trace the letters.

C C C a a a O O O E E E

Cursive write the letters.   Circle your favorites.

Trace the words.

Cal Allen Ollie Enter

Cursive write the words.   Circle your favorites.

Name _____

Introduction to Big Flagpole Letters
n m K H

When writing a big flagpole letter you will begin at the top of the letter, curve upward, and then draw the line down to the bottom line. Practice this stroke by tracing the lines on each flagpole. Start on the ● and end on the ■.

Introduction to Big Flagpole Letters
n m K H

Name _____

When writing a big flagpole letter you will begin at the top of the letter, curve upward, and then draw the line down to the bottom line. Practice this stroke by tracing the lines on each flagpole. Start on the ● and end on the ■.

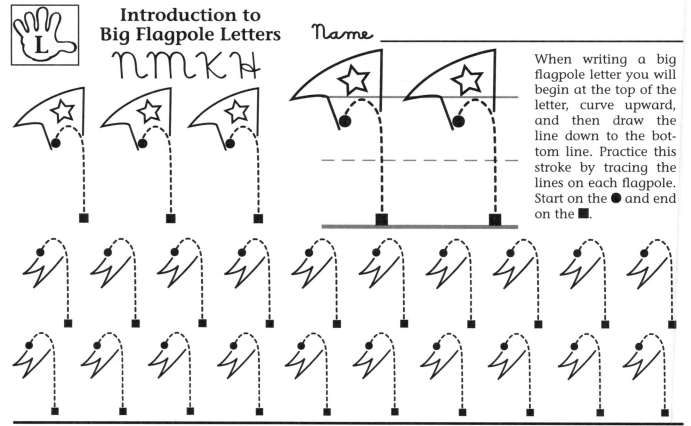

- 108 -

Trace the letters.

Name _____

Level 1 **R**

Rainbow Writing Directions: Trace each letter several times, each time using a different colored crayon.

Trace the letters.

Name _____

Level 1 **R**

Rainbow Writing Directions: Trace each letter several times, each time using a different colored crayon.

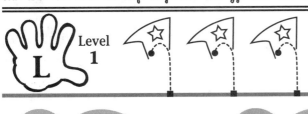

Trace the letters.

Level **L** 1

Name _____

Rainbow Writing Directions: Trace each letter several times, each time using a different colored crayon.

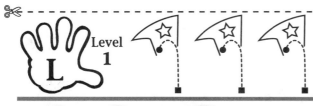

Trace the letters.

Level **L** 1

Name _____

Rainbow Writing Directions: Trace each letter several times, each time using a different colored crayon.

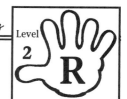

Level 2 R

Learn Letters

n m

Name _____

Meet Nancy Newt and Mary Mouse.

Trace the letters.

n n n n n n n

Cursive write the letters.   Circle your favorite letters.

Circle letters "n" and "m."

n n m t m h m k n

Trace the letters.

m m m m m m m

Cursive write the letters.   Circle your favorite letters.

Level 2

L

Name _____

Meet Nancy Newt and Mary Mouse.

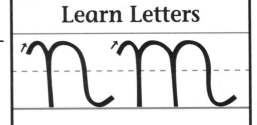

Learn Letters

Trace the letters.

n n n n n n n n n

Cursive write the letters.

Circle your favorite letters.

Circle letters " n " and " m ."

n n m t t m H m k n

Trace the letters.

m m m m m m m m m

Cursive write the letters.

Circle your favorite letters.

n

Name _____

Level 3 **R**

Trace the letters.

Cursive write the letters.

n n n n n

Trace the words.

No Ned Nancy Now

Cursive write the words.

Circle your favorites.

✂ -

Aa Bb Cc Dd Ee Ff Gg Hh Ii Jj Kk Ll Mm Nn Oo Pp Qq Rr Ss Tt Uu Vv Ww Xx Yy Zz

m

Name _____

Level 3 **R**

Trace the letters.

Cursive write the letters.

m m m m

Trace the words.

Mary Mike Mark May

Cursive write the words.

Circle your favorites.

Name _____

Trace the letters.   Cursive write the letters.

n   n   n   n   n

Trace the words.

No   Ned   Nancy   Now

Cursive write the words.   Circle your favorites.

Name _____

Trace the letters.   Cursive write the letters.

m   m   m   m   m

Trace the words.

Mary   Mike   Mark   May

Cursive write the words.   Circle your favorites.

Trace the letters.

Name _____

Level 1 R

Rainbow Writing Directions: Trace each letter several times, each time using a different colored crayon.

Trace the letters.

Name _____

Level 1 R

Rainbow Writing Directions: Trace each letter several times, each time using a different colored crayon.

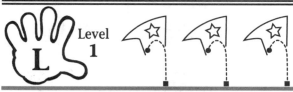
Level 1 L

Trace the letters.

Name _____

1 ↗   2 ↙

K K K K

Rainbow Writing Directions: Trace each letter several times, each time using a different colored crayon.

✂ -

Level 1 L

Trace the letters.

Name _____

1 ↗   ↓ 2

H H H H

Rainbow Writing Directions: Trace each letter several times, each time using a different colored crayon.

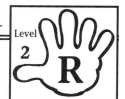

Level 2 R

Learn Letters

K H

Name _____

Ken Koala is Harry Horse's friend.

Trace the letters.

K K K K K K K

Cursive write the letters.

Circle your favorite letters.

Circle letters " K " and " H ."

N K J K H H K M H

Trace the letters.

H H H H H H H H

Cursive write the letters.

Circle your favorite letters.

Level 2

Name _____

Ken Koala is Harry Horse's friend.

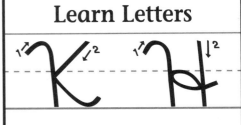

Learn Letters

K   H

Trace the letters.

K K K K K K K

Cursive write the letters.   Circle your favorite letters.

Circle letters " K " and " H."

N K J K H H K M H

Trace the letters.

H H H H H H H

Cursive write the letters.   Circle your favorite letters.

Level 3 R

Name _____

Trace the letters.   Cursive write the letters.

K K K K K

Trace the words.

Ken   Karen   Karl   Kim

Cursive write the words.   Circle your favorites.

✂ -

Level 3 R

Name _____

Trace the letters.   Cursive write the letters.

H H H H H H

Trace the words.

Hat   Hope   Heidi   Harry

Cursive write the words.   Circle your favorites.

Aa Bb Cc Dd Ee Ff Gg Hh Ii Jj Kk Ll Mm Nn Oo Pp 2q Rr Ss Tt Uu Vv Ww Xx Yy Zz

L Level 3

Name _____

K

Trace the letters.

Cursive write the letters.

K K K K K

Trace the words.

Ken Karen Karl Kim

Cursive write the words.

Circle your favorites.

- ✂ -

Aa Bb Cc Dd Ee Ff Gg Hh Ii Jj Kk Ll Mm Nn Oo Pp 2q Rr Ss Tt Uu Vv Ww Xx Yy Zz

L Level 3

Name _____

H

Trace the letters.

Cursive write the letters.

H H H H H H

Trace the words.

Hat Hope Heidi Harry

Cursive write the words.

Circle your favorites.

Name _____

Introduction to Big Letters with a Ball

PBR

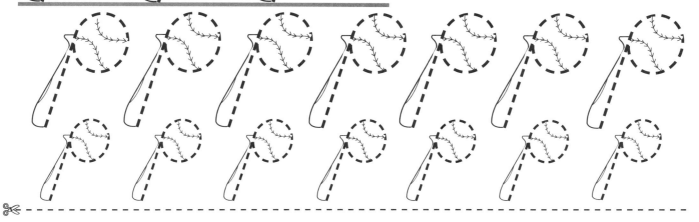

Put your pencil on the ●. Draw a line down the dashed line and then draw a line back up again to the ●. Then, once you are back at the ●, keep going and make a circular shape. This looks like a bat and a ball. First, draw a line for the bat, and then make a circular shape for a ball.

Introduction to Big Letters with a Ball

PBR

Name _____

Put your pencil on the ●. Draw a line straight down the dashed line and then draw a line back up again to the ●. Then, once you are back at the ●, keep going and make a circular shape. This looks like a bat and a ball. First, draw a line for the bat, and then make a circular shape for a ball.

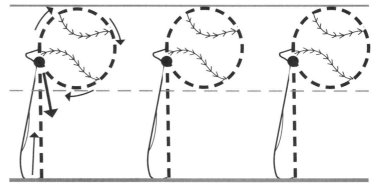

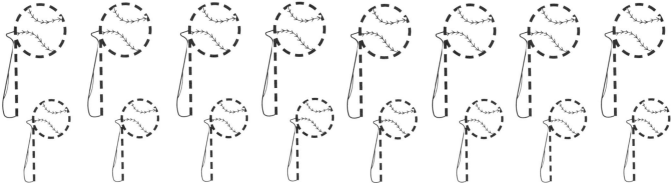

Rainbow Writing Directions: Trace each letter several times, each time using a different colored crayon.

Name

Level 1 **R**

P P P P

Rainbow Writing Directions: Trace each letter several times, each time using a different colored crayon.

Name

Level 1 **R**

B B B B

Rainbow Writing Directions: Trace each letter several times, each time using a different colored crayon.

Name

Level 1 **R**

R R R R

L Level 1

Rainbow Writing Directions: Trace each letter several times, each time using a different colored crayon.

Name

P P P P

Rainbow Writing Directions: Trace each letter several times, each time using a different colored crayon.

L Level 1

Name

B B B B

Rainbow Writing Directions: Trace each letter several times, each time using a different colored crayon.

L Level 1

Name

R R R R

Aa Bb Cc Dd Ee Ff Gg Hh Ii Jj Kk Ll Mm Nn Oo Pp Qq Rr Ss Tt Uu Vv Ww Xx Yy Zz

(Big Ball Letters)

Learn Letters P B R

Level 2 Right-Hand

Name _____

Trace the letters.

P P P P P P P P

Cursive write the letters.   Circle your favorite letters.

Trace the letters.

B B B B B B B B

Cursive write the letters.   Circle your favorite letters.

Trace the letters.

R R R R R R R R

Cursive write the letters.   Circle your favorite letters.

Aa Bb Cc Dd Ee Ff Gg Hh Ii Jj Kk Ll Mm Nn Oo Pp Qq Rr Ss Tt Uu Vv Ww Xx Yy Zz

Level 2 Left-Hand

Name _____

Learn Letters

P B R

Trace the letters.

P P P P P P P P

Cursive write the letters.   Circle your favorite letters.

Trace the letters.

B B B B B B B B

Cursive write the letters.   Circle your favorite letters.

Trace the letters.

R R R R R R R R

Cursive write the letters.   Circle your favorite letters.

Aa Bb Cc Dd Ee Ff Gg Hh Ii Jj Kk Ll Mm Nn Oo Pp 2q Rr Ss Tt Uu Vv Ww Xx Yy Zz

Level 3 Right-Hand

Trace the letters and words.

Name _____

P P P P P P Pam Peter Paul

Cursive write all by yourself.   Circle your favorites.

- -

✂- -

Aa Bb Cc Dd Ee Ff Gg Hh Ii Jj Kk Ll Mm Nn Oo Pp 2q Rr Ss Tt Uu Vv Ww Xx Yy Zz

Level 3 Right-Hand

Name _____

Trace the letters and words.

B B B B Brad Bob Barb

Cursive write all by yourself.   Circle your favorites.

- -

✂- -

Aa Bb Cc Dd Ee Ff Gg Hh Ii Jj Kk Ll Mm Nn Oo Pp 2q Rr Ss Tt Uu Vv Ww Xx Yy Zz

Level 3 Right-Hand

Name _____

Trace the letters and words.

R R R R Rob Rick Reggie

Cursive write all by yourself.   Circle your favorites.

- -

Aa Bb Cc Dd Ee Ff Gg Hh Ii Jj Kk Ll Mm Nn Oo Pp Qq Rr Ss Tt Uu Vv Ww Xx Yy Zz

Left-Hand Level 3

Name _____

P

Trace the letters and words.

P P P P P Pam Peter Paul

Cursive write all by yourself.   Circle your favorites.

Aa Bb Cc Dd Ee Ff Gg Hh Ii Jj Kk Ll Mm Nn Oo Pp Qq Rr Ss Tt Uu Vv Ww Xx Yy Zz

Left-Hand Level 3

Name _____

B

Trace the letters and words.

B B B B Brad Bob Barb

Cursive write all by yourself.   Circle your favorites.

Aa Bb Cc Dd Ee Ff Gg Hh Ii Jj Kk Ll Mm Nn Oo Pp Qq Rr Ss Tt Uu Vv Ww Xx Yy Zz

Left-Hand Level 3

Name _____

R

Trace the letters and words.

R R R R Rob Rick Reggie

Cursive write all by yourself.   Circle your favorites.

R

**Review Big Flagpole Letters
and Big Ball and Bat Letters**

MNKHPBR

Name _____

Trace the letters.

N M K H P B R

Cursive write the letters.　　　　　　　　Circle your favorites.

Trace the words.

No Mic Ken Hi Paul Bob

Cursive write the words.　　　　　　　　Circle your favorites.

✂ -

L

**Review Big Flagpole Letters
and Big Ball and Bat Letters**

MNKHPBR Name _____

Trace the letters.

N M K H P B R

Cursive write the letters.　　　　　　　　Circle your favorites.

Trace the words.

No Mic Ken Hi Paul Bob

Cursive write the words.　　　　　　　　Circle your favorites.

Name _____

Introduction to Big Snake Letters
U W Y V X

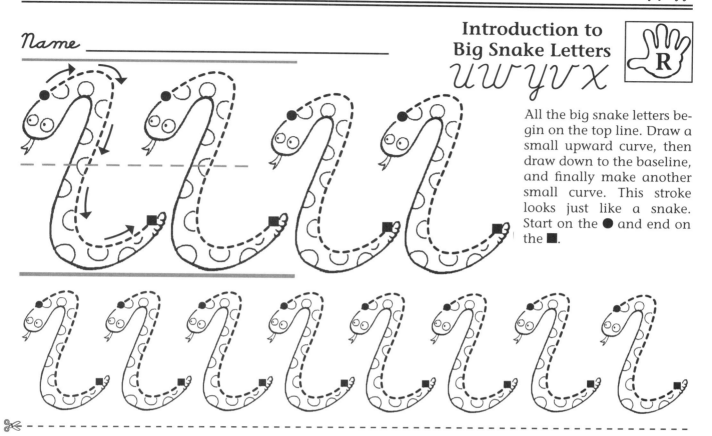

All the big snake letters begin on the top line. Draw a small upward curve, then draw down to the baseline, and finally make another small curve. This stroke looks just like a snake. Start on the ● and end on the ■.

✂ -

Introduction to Big Snake Letters
U W Y V X

Name _____

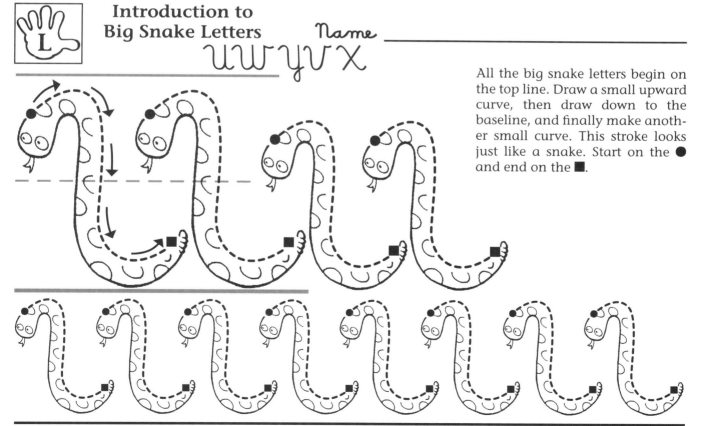

All the big snake letters begin on the top line. Draw a small upward curve, then draw down to the baseline, and finally make another small curve. This stroke looks just like a snake. Start on the ● and end on the ■.

Trace the letters.

Name _____

Level 1 R

u u u

Rainbow Writing Directions: Trace each letter several times, each time using a different colored crayon.

Trace the letters.

Name _____

Level 1 R

w w w

Rainbow Writing Directions: Trace each letter several times, each time using a different colored crayon.

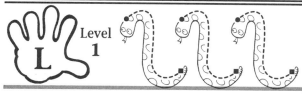

Level
L 1

Trace the letters.

Name _____

Rainbow Writing Directions: Trace each letter several times, each time using a different colored crayon.

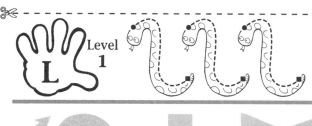

Level
L 1

Trace the letters.

Name _____

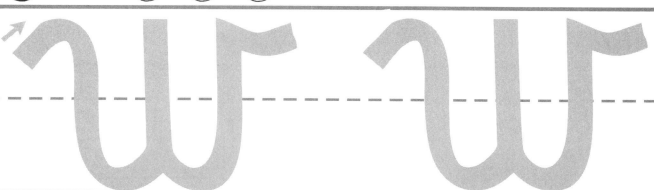

Rainbow Writing Directions: Trace each letter several times, each time using a different colored crayon.

Learn Letters

$\mathcal{U}$ $\mathcal{W}$

Name _____

Wally Walrus likes
Ursula the Uakari Monkey.

Trace the letters.

$\mathcal{U}$ $\mathcal{U}$ $\mathcal{U}$ $\mathcal{U}$ $\mathcal{U}$ $\mathcal{U}$ $\mathcal{U}$ $\mathcal{U}$

Cursive write the letters.   Circle your favorite letters.

Circle letters "$\mathcal{U}$" and "$\mathcal{W}$."

$\mathcal{U}$ $\mathcal{U}$ $\mathcal{X}$ $\mathcal{U}$ $\mathcal{V}$ $\mathcal{W}$ $\mathcal{N}$ $\mathcal{W}$ $\mathcal{W}$

Trace the letters.

$\mathcal{W}$ $\mathcal{W}$ $\mathcal{W}$ $\mathcal{W}$ $\mathcal{W}$ $\mathcal{W}$

Cursive write the letters.   Circle your favorite letters.

L Level 2

Name _____

Wally Walrus likes
Ursula the Uakari Monkey.

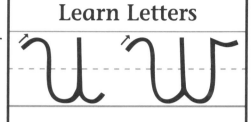

Learn Letters

U W

Trace the letters.

U U U U U U U U U

Cursive write the letters.   Circle your favorite letters.

Circle letters "U" and "W."

U U X X U V W N W W

Trace the letters.

W W W W W

Cursive write the letters.   Circle your favorite letters.

Level 3 R

U

Name _____

Trace the letters.

Cursive write the letters.

U U U U U

Trace the words.

Cursive write the words.

Circle your favorites.

Utah Under Use Up

- -

Level 3 R

W

Name _____

Trace the letters.

Cursive write the letters.

W W W W

Trace the words.

Wendy Water Why Wet

Cursive write the words.

Circle your favorites.

Name _____

Trace the letters.

Cursive write the letters.

U U U U U

Trace the words.

Utah   Under   Use   Up

Cursive write the words.

Circle your favorites.

✂ -

Name _____

Trace the letters.

Cursive write the letters.

W W W W

Trace the words.

Wendy Water Why Wet

Cursive write the words.

Circle your favorites.

Rainbow Writing Directions: Trace each letter several times, each time using a different colored crayon.

Name Level 1

𝒴 𝒴 𝒴 𝒴

Rainbow Writing Directions: Trace each letter several times, each time using a different colored crayon.

Name Level 1

𝒱 𝒱 𝒱

Rainbow Writing Directions: Trace each letter several times, each time using a different colored crayon.

Name Level 1

Rainbow Writing Directions: Trace each letter several times, each time using a different colored crayon.

L Level 1   *Name*

Rainbow Writing Directions: Trace each letter several times, each time using a different colored crayon.

L Level 1   *Name*

Rainbow Writing Directions: Trace each letter several times, each time using a different colored crayon.

L Level 1   *Name*

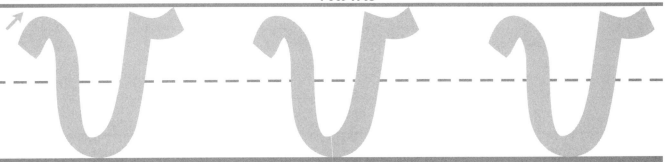

V X Y Learn Letters

Name _____

Trace the letters.

Cursive write the letters.   Circle your favorite letters.

Trace the letters.

Cursive write the letters.   Circle your favorite letters.

Trace the letters.

Cursive write the letters.   Circle your favorite letters.

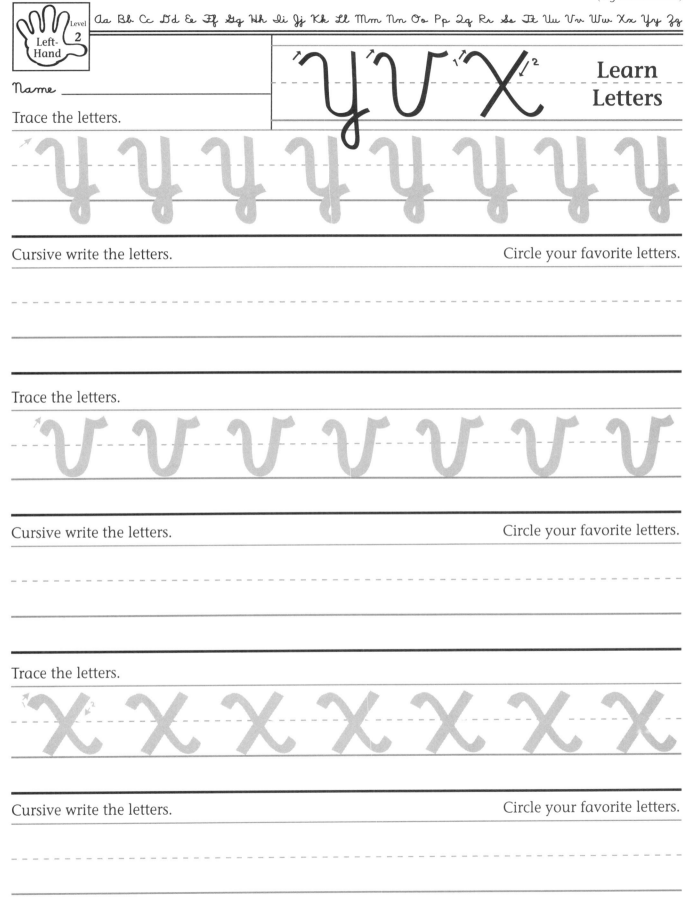

Level 2 — Left-Hand

Aa Bb Cc Dd Ee Ff Gg Hh Ii Jj Kk Ll Mm Nn Oo Pp Qq Rr Ss Tt Uu Vv Ww Xx Yy Zz

Learn Letters

Name _____

Trace the letters.

Cursive write the letters.   Circle your favorite letters.

Trace the letters.

Cursive write the letters.   Circle your favorite letters.

Trace the letters.

Cursive write the letters.   Circle your favorite letters.

Aa Bb Cc Dd Ee Ff Gg Hh Ii Jj Kk Ll Mm Nn Oo Pp Qq Rr Ss Tt Uu Vv Ww Xx Yy Zz

Level 3 Right-Hand

Y

Name _____

Trace the letters and words.

Y Y Y Y Yak Yam Yoke

Cursive write all by yourself.

Circle your favorites.

✂ -

Aa Bb Cc Dd Ee Ff Gg Hh Ii Jj Kk Ll Mm Nn Oo Pp Qq Rr Ss Tt Uu Vv Ww Xx Yy Zz

Level 3 Right-Hand

V

Name _____

Trace the letters and words.

V V V V Van Vase Vince

Cursive write all by yourself.

Circle your favorites.

✂ -

Aa Bb Cc Dd Ee Ff Gg Hh Ii Jj Kk Ll Mm Nn Oo Pp Qq Rr Ss Tt Uu Vv Ww Xx Yy Zz

Level 3 Right-Hand

X

Name _____

Trace the letters and words.

X X X X-ray Xylophone

Cursive write all by yourself.

Circle your favorites.

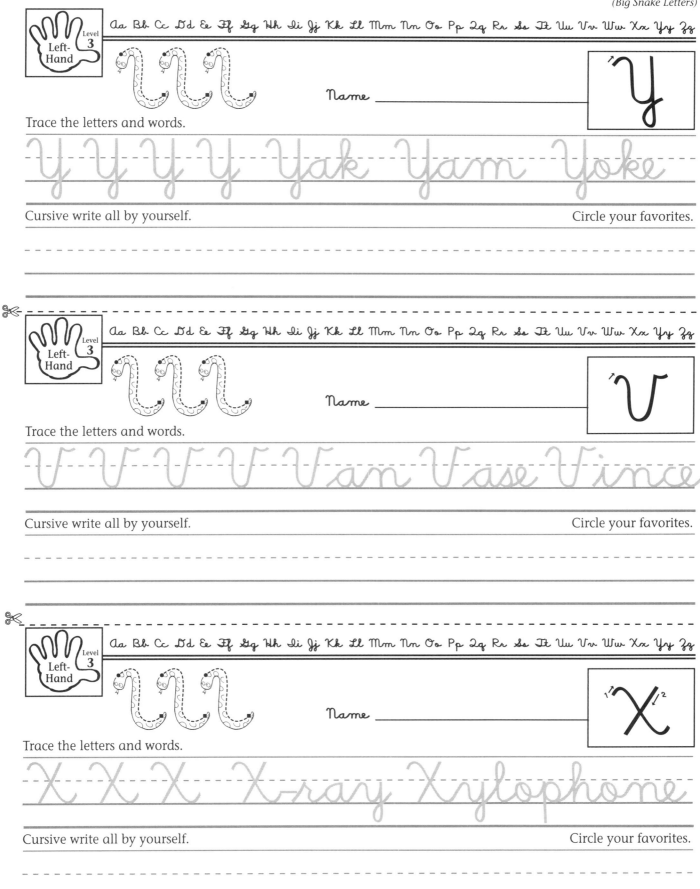

Aa Bb Cc Dd Ee Ff Gg Hh Ii Jj Kk Ll Mm Nn Oo Pp Qq Rr Ss Tt Uu Vv Ww Xx Yy Zz

Left-Hand Level 3

Trace the letters and words.

Name _____

Y Y Y Y Yak Yam Yoke

Cursive write all by yourself.

Circle your favorites.

Aa Bb Cc Dd Ee Ff Gg Hh Ii Jj Kk Ll Mm Nn Oo Pp Qq Rr Ss Tt Uu Vv Ww Xx Yy Zz

Left-Hand Level 3

Trace the letters and words.

Name _____

V V V V V Van Vase Vince

Cursive write all by yourself.

Circle your favorites.

Aa Bb Cc Dd Ee Ff Gg Hh Ii Jj Kk Ll Mm Nn Oo Pp Qq Rr Ss Tt Uu Vv Ww Xx Yy Zz

Left-Hand Level 3

Trace the letters and words.

Name _____

X X X X-ray Xylophone

Cursive write all by yourself.

Circle your favorites.

Aa Bb Cc Dd Ee Ff Gg Hh Ii Jj Kk Ll Mm Nn Oo Pp Qq Rr Ss Tt Uu Vv Ww Xx Yy Zz

Name _____

Introduction to Big Hat Letters
T F

There are two strokes to complete letter "T," and three strokes needed to complete letter "F." Start on the ● s and end on the ■ s.

Aa Bb Cc Dd Ee Ff Gg Hh Ii Jj Kk Ll Mm Nn Oo Pp Qq Rr Ss Tt Uu Vv Ww Xx Yy Zz

Introduction to Big Hat Letters
T F

Name _____

There are two strokes to complete letter "T," and three strokes needed to complete letter "F." Start on the ● s and end on the ■ s.

Trace the letters.

Name _____

Level 1 R

$T\ T\ T$

Rainbow Writing Directions: Trace each letter several times, each time using a different colored crayon.

Trace the letters.

Name _____

Level 1 R

$F\ F\ F$

Rainbow Writing Directions: Trace each letter several times, each time using a different colored crayon.

Level **L** 1

Trace the letters.

Name _____

Rainbow Writing Directions: Trace each letter several times, each time using a different colored crayon.

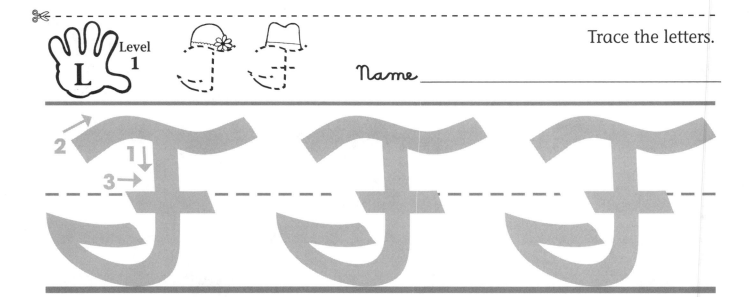

Level **L** 1

Trace the letters.

Name _____

Rainbow Writing Directions: Trace each letter several times, each time using a different colored crayon.

Level 2 R

Learn Letters

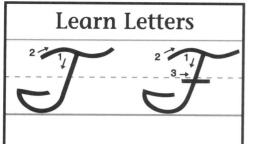

Name _____

Look at Tom Turtle and Fred Fox.

Trace the letters.

Cursive write the letters.   Circle your favorite letters.

Circle letters "T" and "F."

Trace the letters.

Cursive write the letters.   Circle your favorite letters.

Level 2

Name _____

Look at <u>T</u>om <u>T</u>urtle and <u>F</u>red <u>F</u>ox.

Learn Letters

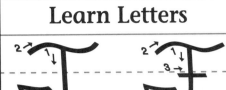

Trace the letters.

T T T T T T T T T

Cursive write the letters.   Circle your favorite letters.

Circle letters " T " and " F."

T F L T T H T K F F

Trace the letters.

F F F F F F F F F

Cursive write the letters.   Circle your favorite letters.

(Big Hat Letters)

Level 3 R

Name _____

Trace the letters.   Cursive write the letters.

T T T T T

Trace the words.

Todd Ted Tim Terri

Cursive write the words.   Circle your favorites.

✂ -

Aa Bb Cc Dd Ee Ff Gg Hh Ii Jj Kk Ll Mm Nn Oo Pp 2q Rr Ss Tt Uu Vv Ww Xx Yy Zz

Level 3 R

Name _____

Trace the letters.   Cursive write the letters.

F F F F F

Trace the words.

Fran Fred Friday Fix

Cursive write the words.   Circle your favorites.

Aa Bb Cc Dd Ee Ff Gg Hh Ii Jj Kk Ll Mm Nn Oo Pp Qq Rr Ss Tt Uu Vv Ww Xx Yy Zz

L Level 3

Name _____

$\mathcal{T}$

Trace the letters.

$\mathcal{T}$ $\mathcal{T}$ $\mathcal{T}$ $\mathcal{T}$ $\mathcal{T}$ $\mathcal{T}$

Cursive write the letters.

Trace the words.

Todd Ted Tim Terri

Cursive write the words.

Circle your favorites.

✂ -

Aa Bb Cc Dd Ee Ff Gg Hh Ii Jj Kk Ll Mm Nn Oo Pp Qq Rr Ss Tt Uu Vv Ww Xx Yy Zz

L Level 3

Name _____

$\mathcal{F}$

Trace the letters.

$\mathcal{F}$ $\mathcal{F}$ $\mathcal{F}$ $\mathcal{F}$ $\mathcal{F}$

Cursive write the letters.

Trace the words.

Fran Fred Friday Fix

Cursive write the words.

Circle your favorites.

R

Review Big Snake Letters and Big Hat Letters

U W Y V X T F

Name _____

Trace the letters.

U   W   Y   V   X   T   F

Cursive write the letters.   Circle your favorites.

Trace the words.

Up Will Yak Van To For

Cursive write the words.   Circle your favorites.

L

Aa Bb Cc Dd Ee Ff Gg Hh Ii Jj Kk Ll Mm Nn Oo Pp Qq Rr Ss Tt Uu Vv Ww Xx Yy Zz

Review Big Snake Letters and Big Hat Letters

U W Y V X T F

Name _____

Trace the letters.

U   W   Y   V   X   T   F

Cursive write the letters.   Circle your favorites.

Trace the words.

Up Will Yak Van To For

Cursive write the words.   Circle your favorites.

Name _____

Introduction to
Big Curly Letters

2 z L J G S L D

In each of the big curly letters there is a "curl" or "loop." This page provides practice in drawing "curls" and "loops." Begin drawing on the ○ and end on the ▲.

Introduction to
Big Curly Letters

2 z L J G S L D

Name _____

In each of the big curly letters there is a "curl" or "loop." This page provides practice in drawing "curls" and "loops." Begin drawing on the ○ and end on the ▲.

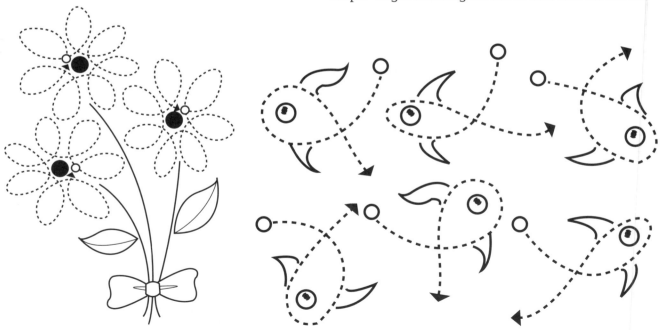

Trace the letters.

Name _____

Level 1 R

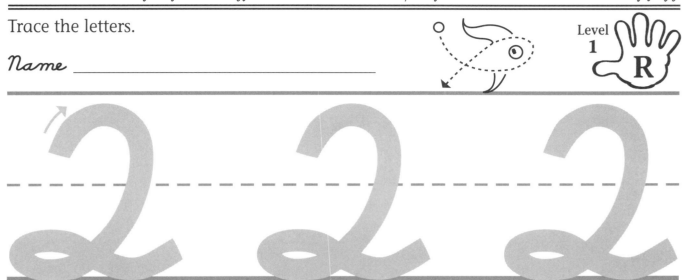

Rainbow Writing Directions: Trace each letter several times, each time using a different colored crayon.

Trace the letters.

Name _____

Level 1 R

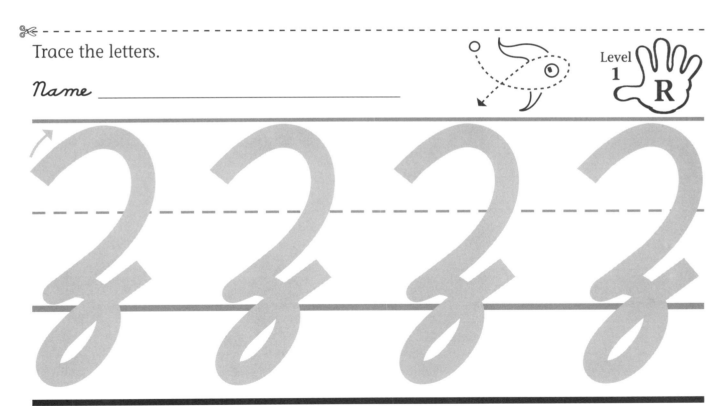

Rainbow Writing Directions: Trace each letter several times, each time using a different colored crayon.

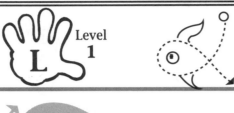

Level 1

Trace the letters.

Name _____

Rainbow Writing Directions: Trace each letter several times, each time using a different colored crayon.

Level 1

Trace the letters.

Name _____

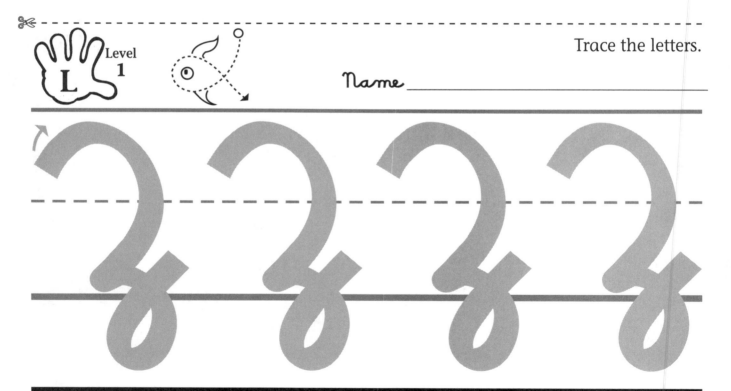

Rainbow Writing Directions: Trace each letter several times, each time using a different colored crayon.

Level 2 R

Learn Letters

2 Z

Name _____

Zelda Zebra
bows to Queen Quail.

Trace the letters.

2 2 2 2 2 2 2 2 2

Cursive write the letters.   Circle your favorite letters.

Circle letters "2" and "Z."

2 L 2 Z J 2 Z Y Z

Trace the letters.

Z Z Z Z Z Z Z Z Z

Cursive write the letters.   Circle your favorite letters.

Level 2 **L**

Name _____

Learn Letters

Zelda Zebra
bows to Queen Quail.

Trace the letters.

Cursive write the letters.

Circle your favorite letters.

Circle letters "2" and "Z."

Trace the letters.

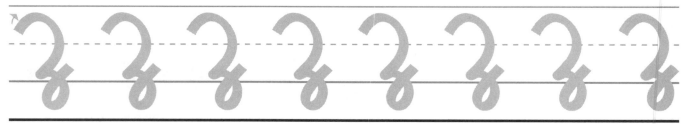

Cursive write the letters.

Circle your favorite letters.

Level 3 R

Q

Name _____

Trace the letters.   Cursive write the letters.

Q Q Q Q Q

Trace the words.

Quit Queen Quiet Quail

Cursive write the words.   Circle your favorites.

✂ -

Level 3 R

Z

Name _____

Trace the letters.   Cursive write the letters.

Z Z Z Z Z

Trace the words.

Zoo Zebra Zipper Zap

Cursive write the words.   Circle your favorites.

(Big Curly Letters)

Aa Bb Cc Dd Ee Ff Gg Hh Ii Jj Kk Ll Mm Nn Oo Pp Qq Rr Ss Tt Uu Vv Ww Xx Yy Zz

Name _____

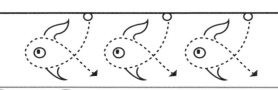

Q

Trace the letters.   Cursive write the letters.

Q Q Q Q Q

Trace the words.

Quit Queen Quiet Quail

Cursive write the words.   Circle your favorites.

- -

Level L 3

Aa Bb Cc Dd Ee Ff Gg Hh Ii Jj Kk Ll Mm Nn Oo Pp Qq Rr Ss Tt Uu Vv Ww Xx Yy Zz

Name _____

Z

Trace the letters.   Cursive write the letters.

Z Z Z Z Z

Trace the words.

Zoo Zebra Zipper Zap

Cursive write the words.   Circle your favorites.

Aa Bb Cc Dd Ee Ff Gg Hh Ii Jj Kk Ll Mm Nn Oo Pp Qq Rr Ss Tt Uu Vv Ww Xx Yy Zz

Trace the letters.

Name _____

Level 1
R

Rainbow Writing Directions: Trace each letter several times, each time using a different colored crayon.

Trace the letters.

Name _____

Level 1
R

Rainbow Writing Directions: Trace each letter several times, each time using a different colored crayon.

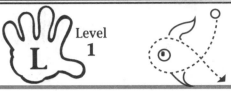

Level 1

Trace the letters.

Name _____

Rainbow Writing Directions: Trace each letter several times, each time using a different colored crayon.

Level 1

Trace the letters.

Name _____

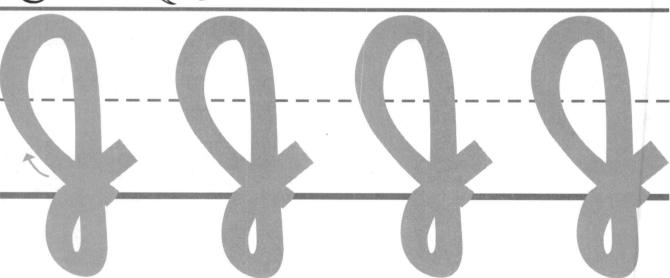

Rainbow Writing Directions: Trace each letter several times, each time using a different colored crayon.

Level 2 R

Learn Letters

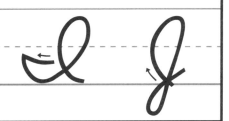

Name _____

Iggie Iguana plays with Jack Jaguar.

Trace the letters.

ℒ ℒ ℒ ℒ ℒ ℒ ℒ

Cursive write the letters.

Circle your favorite letters.

Circle letters "ℒ" and "𝒥."

ℒ ℒ ℒ 𝒥 𝒴 𝒥 𝒥 ℨ ℒ

Trace the letters.

𝒥 𝒥 𝒥 𝒥 𝒥 𝒥 𝒥 𝒥 𝒥

Cursive write the letters.

Circle your favorite letters.

Level L 2

Name _____

Iggie Iguana plays with Jack Jaguar.

Learn Letters

Trace the letters.

Cursive write the letters.   Circle your favorite letters.

Circle letters "L" and "J."

Trace the letters.

Cursive write the letters.   Circle your favorite letters.

Level
3
R

Name _____

Trace the letters.

Cursive write the letters.

I I I I I

Trace the words.

Is It In Ice Ilene

Cursive write the words.

Circle your favorites.

- -

Aa Bb Cc Dd Ee Ff Gg Hh Ii Jj Kk Ll Mm Nn Oo Pp 2q Rr Ss Tt Uu Vv Ww Xx Yy Zz

Level
3
R

Name _____

Trace the letters.

Cursive write the letters.

J J J J J

Trace the words.

Jim Jetty Jack James

Cursive write the words.

Circle your favorites.

L Level 3

Name

Trace the letters.

Cursive write the letters.

ℓ ℓ ℓ ℓ ℓ

Trace the words.

Is It In Ice Ilene

Cursive write the words.

Circle your favorites.

✂ -

L Level 3

Name

Trace the letters.

Cursive write the letters.

J J J J J

Trace the words.

Jim Jelly Jack James

Cursive write the words.

Circle your favorites.

Trace the letters.

Name _____

Level 1 R

Rainbow Writing Directions: Trace each letter several times, each time using a different colored crayon.

Trace the letters.

Name _____

Level 1 R

Rainbow Writing Directions: Trace each letter several times, each time using a different colored crayon.

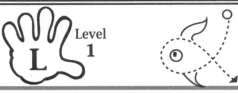

Level 1

Trace the letters.

Name _____

Rainbow Writing Directions: Trace each letter several times, each time using a different colored crayon.

Level 1

Trace the letters.

Name _____

Rainbow Writing Directions: Trace each letter several times, each time using a different colored crayon.

Level 2 R

Learn Letters

Name _____

Gerald Giraffe and
Sam Snake are skinny!

Trace the letters.

Cursive write the letters.   Circle your favorite letters.

Circle letters "G" and "S."

Trace the letters.

Cursive write the letters.   Circle your favorite letters.

L Level 2

Name _____

Gerald Giraffe and
Sam Snake are skinny!

Learn Letters

Trace the letters.

Cursive write the letters.

Circle your favorite letters.

Circle letters "G" and "S."

G U S S L G G 2 S

Trace the letters.

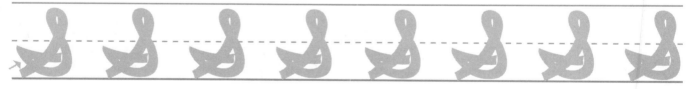

Cursive write the letters.

Circle your favorite letters.

(Big Curly Letters)

Aa Bb Cc Dd Ee Ff Gg Hh Ii Jj Kk Ll Mm Nn Oo Pp 2q Rr Ss Tt Uu Vv Ww Xx Yy Zz

Name _____

Trace the letters.   Cursive write the letters.

G G G G G G

Trace the words.

Go Gone Gerry George

Cursive write the words.   Circle your favorites.

✂ -

Aa Bb Cc Dd Ee Ff Gg Hh Ii Jj Kk Ll Mm Nn Oo Pp 2q Rr Ss Tt Uu Vv Ww Xx Yy Zz

Level 3 R

Name _____

Trace the letters.   Cursive write the letters.

S S S S S S

Trace the words.

Sher Sue Steve Sally

Cursive write the words.   Circle your favorites.

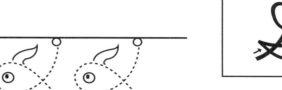

(Big Curly Letters)

Aa Bb Cc Dd Ee Ff Gg Hh Ii Jj Kk Ll Mm Nn Oo Pp Qq Rr Ss Tt Uu Vv Ww Xx Yy Zz

Level 3

Name _____

Trace the letters.

Cursive write the letters.

G G G G G G

Trace the words.

Go Gone Gerry George

Cursive write the words.

Circle your favorites.

✂ -

Level 3

Aa Bb Cc Dd Ee Ff Gg Hh Ii Jj Kk Ll Mm Nn Oo Pp Qq Rr Ss Tt Uu Vv Ww Xx Yy Zz

Name _____

Trace the letters.

Cursive write the letters.

S S S S S S

Trace the words.

Sher Sue Steve Sally

Cursive write the words.

Circle your favorites.

Trace the letters.

Name _____

Level
1
R

Rainbow Writing Directions: Trace each letter several times, each time using a different colored crayon.

Trace the letters.

Name _____

Level
1
R

Rainbow Writing Directions: Trace each letter several times, each time using a different colored crayon.

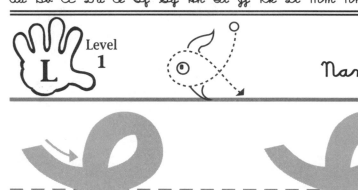

Level 1

Trace the letters.

Name _____

Rainbow Writing Directions: Trace each letter several times, each time using a different colored crayon.

Level 1

Trace the letters.

Name _____

Rainbow Writing Directions: Trace each letter several times, each time using a different colored crayon.

Level 2 R

Learn Letters

Name _____

Did Dave Dog lick Liz Lizard?

Trace the letters.

$\mathcal{L}$ $\mathcal{L}$ $\mathcal{L}$ $\mathcal{L}$ $\mathcal{L}$ $\mathcal{L}$ $\mathcal{L}$ $\mathcal{L}$

Cursive write the letters.

Circle your favorite letters.

Circle letters "$\mathcal{L}$" and "$\mathcal{D}$."

Trace the letters.

$\mathcal{D}$ $\mathcal{D}$ $\mathcal{D}$ $\mathcal{D}$ $\mathcal{D}$ $\mathcal{D}$ $\mathcal{D}$ $\mathcal{D}$

Cursive write the letters.

Circle your favorite letters.

Level 2

Name _____

Did Dave Dog lick Liz Lizard?

Learn Letters

Trace the letters.

Cursive write the letters.

Circle your favorite letters.

Circle letters " L " and " D."

L D 2 L G L D S D

Trace the letters.

Cursive write the letters.

Circle your favorite letters.

Cursive Writing for Right- and Left-Handed Kids

Level
3
R

L

Name _____

Trace the letters.   Cursive write the letters.

L L L L L

Trace the words.

Luke   Lara   Lori   Lark

Cursive write the words.   Circle your favorites.

✂ -

Aa Bb Cc Dd Ee Ff Gg Hh Ii Jj Kk Ll Mm Nn Oo Pp 2q Rr Ss Tt Uu Vv Ww Xx Yy Zz

Level
3
R

D

Name _____

Trace the letters.   Cursive write the letters.

D D D D D

Trace the words.

Dave   Date   Dog   Deidre

Cursive write the words.   Circle your favorites.

Level 3

Name _____

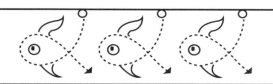

L

Trace the letters.

Cursive write the letters.

L L L L L

Trace the words.

 Luke Lara Lori Lark

Cursive write the words.

Circle your favorites.

Level 3

Name _____

D

Trace the letters.

Cursive write the letters.

D D D D D

Trace the words.

 Dave  Date  Dog Deidre

Cursive write the words.

Circle your favorites.

Cursive Writing for Right- and Left-Handed Kids

Review
Big Curly Letters

Q Z I J G S L D

R

Name _____

Trace the letters.

Q   Z   I   J   G   S   L   D

Cursive write the letters.   Circle your favorites.

Trace the words.

Zoo Is Jim Go So Lie Do

Cursive write the words.   Circle your favorites.

L

Review
Big Curly Letters

Name _____

Q Z I J G S L D

Trace the letters.

Q   Z   I   J   G   S   L   D

Cursive write the letters.   Circle your favorites.

Trace the words.

Zoo Is Jim Go So Lie Do

Cursive write the words.   Circle your favorites.

Aa Bb Cc Dd Ee Ff Gg Hh Ii Jj Kk Ll Mm Nn Oo Pp Qq Rr Ss Tt Uu Vv Ww Xx Yy Zz

Handwriting Assessment Form

Directions: The Handwriting Assessment Form can be used to document student progress. The teacher can chose how often to record the data. Have the students cursive write the sentence, "The quick brown fox jumps over the lazy dog." This sentence uses every alphabet letter. Have the children write the sentence in lowercase and capital letters.

Student's Name: _____

Date	Pencil Grasp/ Posture	LOWERCASE Little Letters i, t, u, w	LOWERCASE More Little Letters r, s, p, j	LOWERCASE Little Round Letters c, o, a, d, g, q	LOWERCASE Little Hill Letters n, m, v, x, y, z	LOWERCASE Little Tall Letters e, l, h, b, k, f	UPPERCASE Big Round Letters C, A, O, E	UPPERCASE Big Flagpole Letters N, M, K, H	UPPERCASE Big Letters with a Ball P, B, R	UPPERCASE Big Snake Letters U, W, V, X	UPPERCASE Big Letters with a Hat T, F	UPPERCASE Big Curly Letters Q, Z, I, J	UPPERCASE More Big Curly Letters G, S, L, D	Letter Spacing/ Slant	Word Spacing/ Margins	Additional Comments